THE
HOUSEHOLD
HANDBOOK

Answers and Solutions You Need to Know

**by the
Meadowbrook Reference Group**

Meadowbrook Press
18318 Minnetonka Boulevard
Deephaven, Minnesota 55391

First printing November 1981

Printed in the United States of America

Library of Congress Cataloging in Publication Data

Main entry under title:

The Household handbook.

Includes bibliographical references and index.
1. Home economics—Handbooks, manuals, etc.

I. Grady, Tom, 1951 –   II. Rood, Amy,
1956 –
TX158.H647   640   81 – 17226
ISBN 0 – 915658—46 – 1   AACR2
ISBN 0 – 915668—41 – 0 (pbk.)

ISBN (paperback): 0–915658–41–0
ISBN (hardcover): 0–915658–46–1

Director: Bruce Lansky
Editor: Tom Grady
Asst. Editor: Amy Rood
Research: Louise Delagran, Mary Grady
Designer: Terry Dugan
Design Assistant: Sandra Falls
Production Manager: John Ware
Illustrator: RMR Portfolio
Consulting Editor: Kathe Grooms

Acknowledgements: Special thanks to Carol Andruskiewicz, Mary Jo Asmus, Nancy Giovinco, Jeff Herpers, Sharon Herpers, Kay Hunke, Debbie Hvass, Jennifer Olson and Nancy Palesch.

Contents

You've just cut yourself, but you can't remember where you put your first aid manual. You've run out of sour cream, and you can't remember which of your cookbooks has a substitutions chart in it. You've spilled wine on your carpet—where's that stain-removal chart you cut out of a magazine? It's tornado season and you remember reading about how to protect yourself in one, but what *are* those safety rules? One of your plants droops—should you give it more water or more light? How long can that fish you caught last week stay in the freezer?

The Household Handbook answers dozens of questions, solves hundreds of problems and gives you more practical information than ten other books combined. It's a collection of the most *useful* and *authoritative* information you can get on dozens of subjects you need to know something about—from cooking, nutrition, and first aid to housekeeping, houseplants, home repairs and home security. A whole library of books is condensed into one volume!

• It's *useful* because the information is presented in the most practical, easy-to-comprehend ways possible. *The Household Handbook* is full of hundreds of charts, tables and lists. You find what you need quickly, and you understand it at a glance.

• It's *authoritative* because the information comes from organizations that know what they're talking about: the National Weather Service, the National Fire Protection Association, the Departments of Agriculture and Energy, the American Medical Association, the National Fisheries Institute, Metropolitan Life Insurance, and many others. There's no folk wisdom here—it's tried and tested advice.

Open this book to any page and you'll find yourself learning something new or remembering something you've learned before about the basics of running a house. Keep it handy—you'll be using it often.

Chapter 1

CLEANING YOUR HOUSE

🧹 Removing Stains

While the *procedures* for removing stains from fabrics and from carpets and rugs are often different, the *materials* used are often the same. Below is a list of the supplies you should have on hand to remove stains, as well as some general tips for stain removal. The two charts that follow offer specific instructions.

Supplies checklist

☐ Blotting materials (paper towels, facial tissues, paper napkins, bath towels, white sheets, soft cloth)
☐ Ammonia
☐ Bar soap
☐ Chlorine bleach
☐ Drycleaning fluid (Carbona, Energine, K2r)
☐ Lemon juice
☐ Liquid hand dishwashing detergent
☐ Rubbing alcohol
☐ Turpentine
☐ White vinegar

Stain removal tips

• **Pretesting.** Test the stain removal treatment you plan to use on an inconspicuous portion of the fabric or carpet to be sure it won't hurt the material. Call a professional drycleaner or carpet cleaner for advice if dyes bleed or the fiber changes appearance.

• **Treatment.** Treat fabric or carpet gently. Don't rub or dab heavily at the problem area. For carpets and non-washable fabrics, apply a small amount of cleaner and work gently from the edges of the soiled area to avoid spreading the spot or stain.

FABRIC CHART

Stain	How to Remove
Grease, oil, ice cream, chocolate, gravy, egg, mayonnaise	• Run cool water over stained area, rub with liquid detergent, and then soak. Rinse and wash as you normally would. • If stain persists, rub with drycleaning solution; rinse and wash. Repeat if necessary.
Chewing gum, candle wax, adhesive tape	• Rub with ice to harden. Scrape area with fingernail or dull knife. • Wipe remaining stain with a drycleaning solvent. Let dry and then wash. • If the color of the stain remains after soaking, use a bleach* in the wash.

*Always check the care label of each item to make sure chlorine bleach is safe to use. If it is not, use an all-fabric bleach.

FABRIC CHART

Stain	How to Remove
Blood	• Soak immediately in cold water. If stain has set, soak for at least 45 min. • Rub with bar soap and then wash. • If stain persists, soak in a solution of 3 tsp. ammonia to 1 qt. cold water and then wash, using chlorine bleach.*
Milk, vomit	• Soak in a solution of 1 cup salt to 1 gal. cool water; rinse and wash. • If stain persists, apply a few drops of ammonia; rinse and wash.
Wine, liquor	• Soak in cool water. Then sponge with white vinegar. Rinse well and wash.
Catsup, tomato sauce, baby formula	• Soak in warm water with liquid dishwashing detergent and a drop of ammonia. Rinse and wash, using a bleach.*
Perspiration	• Rub with liquid detergent, rinse and wash. • If stain persists, apply ammonia or white vinegar; rinse and wash.
Urine	• Soak in a solution of equal parts white vinegar and cool water. • Wash with detergent and cool water; rinse well with clear, cool water.
Water spots	• Sponge entire stained area with white vinegar; let stand a few minutes. Rinse with clear, cool water and let dry.
Grass	• Sponge with liquid detergent and rinse. • If stain persists apply rubbing alcohol; rinse and wash.

*Always check the care label of each item to make sure chlorine bleach is safe to use. If it is not, use an all-fabric bleach.

◢ Removing Stains from Fabrics

FABRIC CHART

Stain	How to Remove
Mildew	• Scrape off mildew with fingernail or dull knife. Then wash with mild suds and sponge with alcohol. Rinse and dry. • Or wash in a bleach.* • Or rub on salt and lemon juice and let dry in sun; then rinse and dry.
Yellowing	• Soak in a solution of ½ c. chlorine bleach* and 1 tbsp. white vinegar to 1 gal. warm water. Rinse thoroughly and wash. • If stain persists, repeat treatment and let dry in sun.
Rust	• Rub with lemon juice. Let dry and then wash. • *Never* use chlorine bleach, as it will permanently set the stain.
Ballpoint pen ink	• Put an absorbent pad under the stain and blot the stain with rubbing alcohol, moving the pad frequently to a clean section and blotting until you can't get out any more ink. • Then wash, using chlorine bleach.*
Lipstick, liquid make-up, mascara	• Soak in drycleaning solution and let dry. Rinse and then wash.
Paint, varnish	• Wash out paints and varnishes *before* they dry. Soak in turpentine (unless fabric is acetate). Rinse and wash, using extra detergent.

*Always check the care label of each item to make sure chlorine bleach is safe to use. If it is not, use an all-fabric bleach.

Sources: U.S. Dept. of Agriculture; New York State Cooperative Extension Service; *Dress Better for Less,* Vicki Audette (Meadowbrook Press, 1981).

CARPET CHART

Stain	How to Remove
Alcoholic beverages, black coffee or tea, fruit juices, soft drinks, syrup, washable ink	• Blot up spilled liquid; apply detergent solution (1 tsp. detergent to 1 cup cool water). Cool water without detergent may be effective in removing fresh stains. • When stain has been removed as completely as possible, rinse area with clean, cool water. Blot up excess liquid and dry rug or carpet.
Butter, cooking oil, hand cream, machine oil, some ball point inks	• Blot up or scrape off excess substance. • Apply liquid drycleaning solvent with clean cloth or absorbent cotton. Continue until stain is removed. • Dry rug or carpet and gently brush pile. • Or spray aerosol-type solvent, let dry and vacuum up white powdery residue.
Blood, chocolate, coffee or tea with cream, egg, gravy, ice cream, milk, salad dressing	• Blot up or scrape off excess substance. • Apply drycleaning solvent, followed by detergent solution (1 tsp. detergent to 1 cup cool water).
Animal urine	• Blot up the puddle as much as possible. • Apply several applications of clean, lukewarm water. • Then apply a solution of half white vinegar and half cool water. • Blot up excess liquid, rinse with clear water, and let spot dry. • If stain remains, apply vinegar solution and allow to remain on the stain for about 15 min. Blot up, rinse, and dry carpet.
Cigarette burns	• For small burns on *wool pile,* use small, sharp scissors to carefully snip away charred fibers. Then apply detergent solution; rinse and dry rug or carpet. • *Manufactured fibers* melt and cannot be repaired by this method. Usually it is necessary to cut out the burned area and replace it with a patch. In some textures, the patch will be invisible.

Note: For nail polish, rust, dye and paint stains contact a professional rug and carpet cleaner.

Source: Cooperative Extension Service of the Northeast States.

🧹 19 Uses for Vinegar

Use	Amount	What to Do
KITCHEN		
Cutting grease	A few drops of white vinegar	• When washing an item that is greasy or smelly, add white vinegar to the cleaning water to cut down on the grease and remove the odor.
Removing stains	Equal mixture of salt and white vinegar	• Salt and white vinegar will clean coffee and tea stains from china cups.
Cleaning glassware	½ cup white vinegar to 1 gal. water	• White vinegar added to rinse water will eliminate dull soap film from glassware and make it shine.
Freshening lunch boxes	Small amount of white vinegar	• Dampen a piece of fresh bread with white vinegar and put it in the lunch box overnight.
Cleaning stainless steel	Small amount of white vinegar	• Remove spots on your stainless-steel kitchen equipment by rubbing them with a cloth dampened with white vinegar.
Loosening tough stains	¼ cup white vinegar to 2 cups water	• To loosen hard-to-clean stains in glass, aluminum or porcelain pots or pans, boil white vinegar with water in pan. Wash in hot, soapy water.
Soaking pots and pans	Full-strength white vinegar	• Soak normal food-stained pots and pans in white vinegar for 30 min. • Rinse in hot, soapy water.

19 Uses for Vinegar 🧹

Use	Amount	What to Do
KITCHEN		
Eliminating cooking odors	1 tbsp. white vinegar to 1 cup water	• Boil white vinegar in water to eliminate unpleasant cooking odors.
Handling onions	Small amount of white vinegar	• Rub a little white vinegar on your fingers before and after slicing onions to remove the odor of onions quickly.
Cleaning jars	Small amount of white vinegar	• Rinse the peanut butter and mayonnaise jars you save with white vinegar to eliminate the odor of the former contents.
LAUNDRY		
Rinsing clothes	1 cup white vinegar	• Put a little white vinegar in your last rinse water to make sure your clothes get a thorough rinse.
Fluffing blankets	2 cups white vinegar	• Add white vinegar to a washer tub of water to make a good rinse for both cotton and wool blankets.
Removing deodorant stains	Small amount of white vinegar	• Get rid of stains left by deodorants and antiperspirants on washables by lightly rubbing with white vinegar. • Then launder as usual.

🧹 19 Uses for Vinegar

Use	Amount	What to Do
GENERAL		
Cleaning electric irons	Equal amounts of white or cider vinegar and salt	• Remove dark or burned stains from an electric iron by rubbing with white or cider vinegar and salt, heated first in a small aluminum pan. • Polish in the same way you do silver.
Rubbing varnished wood	1 tsp. white vinegar to 1 qt. lukewarm water	• Renew the luster of varnished surfaces by rubbing them with a soft, lintless cloth wrung out from a solution of white vinegar in lukewarm water. • When rubbing, follow the grain of the wood. • Finish the job by wiping the surface with a soft, dry cloth.
Eliminating tobacco odors	Small bowl of white vinegar	• Eliminate odors in smoke-filled rooms during and after a party by placing a small bowl of white vinegar in the room.
Removing fruit stains	Small amount of white vinegar	• Remove fruit stains from your hands by rubbing them with a little white vinegar; then wipe with a cloth.
Eliminating paint odors	Small bowl of white vinegar	• Absorb the odor of fresh paint by putting a small dish of white vinegar in the room.
Removing decals	Several applications of white vinegar	• Remove old decals by simply painting them with several coats of white vinegar. Give the vinegar time to soak in. • After several min., the decals should wash off easily.

Source: The Vinegar Institute.

- **Paste:** Mix 3 parts baking soda to 1 part water.
- **Solution:** Dissolve 4 tbsp. baking soda in 1 qt. of water.
- **Dry:** Sprinkle baking soda straight from the box.

Use	Amount	What to Do
KITCHEN		
Deodorizing refrigerator	1 box (1 lb.) every other month	• Tear off the top of the box, and place open in the back of the refrigerator or in a shelf on the door.
Deodorizing dishwasher	1 small handful daily	• Save water and energy by running dishwasher only after the evening meal. Once in the morning, before adding soiled dishes, sprinkle baking soda over the bottom of machine. It will absorb odors all day.
Freshening drains, garbage disposal	1 box (previously used in refrigerator)	• When a fresh box of baking soda goes into the refrigerator, recycle the contents of the old box down the drains to keep them sweet and fresh-smelling.
Soaking cooking utensils	Solution	• Let pots and pans soak in hot or warm solution; then wash. • Baking soda cleans glass, porcelain enamel and metal cookware without scratching.
Scouring burned or baked-on foods	Sprinkle dry as needed/ paste	• Scrub with baking soda sprinkled on a plastic scouring pad; rinse and dry. • Or let warm paste soak on burned area; keep wet, then scrub as needed.

⛏ 15 Uses for Baking Soda

Use	Amount	What to Do
KITCHEN		
Shining silver flatware/ serving pieces	Paste	• Mix paste in small bowl and apply with a damp sponge or soft cloth. • Rub until clean; rinse and buff to a shiny gloss.
Sweetening and removing stains from coffee and teapot	Solution/dry	• Wash in solution to remove build-up of coffee oils and tea stains for better tasting brew. • To remove stained areas, shake baking soda on damp cloth or sponge. Rub until clean; rinse and dry.
Freshening coolers, plastic food containers	Solution	• Shake solution in bottle, or sponge out interior, and rinse with clear water to sweeten and clean.
BATHROOM		
Cleaning fiberglass shower stalls	Dry	• Sprinkle on damp sponge and gently scour to clean, deodorize and help remove mildew. Baking soda will not scratch the surface.
Cleaning bathtubs, toilets, tile, chrome	Dry/paste	• Shake on damp sponge and rub soiled areas until clean; rinse and buff dry. • For textured surfaces, apply paste and allow to set a few minutes. Sponge rinse and clean.

Use	Amount	What to Do
GENERAL		
Deodorizing cat litter	1 part baking soda to 3 parts litter	• Cover bottom of litter pan with 1 part baking soda; then cover baking soda with 3 parts litter to absorb odors for up to a week. Litter won't need replacing as often.
Improving septic system	1 cup per week	• Baking soda poured down a toilet or any household drain in the recommended amount makes the average tank of 300–750 gallons work better.
Putting out fire	Dry	• Toss handfuls at the base of flames in the event of grease, oil or electrical fires. • Do not use to put out flames in deep-fat fryers, since this could cause the grease to spatter and the fire to spread.
Deodorizing carpet, rug	Dry	• Test for color fastness in an inconspicuous area. • Sprinkle baking soda dry from the box; allow to set overnight, then vacuum.
Freshening laundry	⅓ cup	• Add baking soda to wash or rinse cycle. Clothes will be sweeter- and cleaner-smelling.

Source: Arm & Hammer, Division of Church & Dwight Co., Inc.

Cleaning Cookware and Utensils

Type of Material	How to Clean
Stainless steel	• Wash by hand in hot, sudsy water or in dishwasher. Rinse and buff dry to remove water spots. • Rub burned-on foods with baking soda or a paste made of ammonia, water and a mild, non-chlorinated scouring powder.
Aluminum	• Hand washing is preferable; or wash in dishwasher, but turn it off before the drying cycle begins. • To remove stains and discolorations, boil a solution of 2–3 tbsp. of cream of tartar, lemon juice or vinegar added to 1 qt. of water in the utensil for 5–10 min.; then lightly scour with a soap-filled pad.
Cast iron	• Wash in hot, soapy water; rinse and dry immediately. Never use strong detergents or scouring powders. Never store with lid on. Remove rust with steel wool. • To season, coat with unsalted oil or shortening, heat in moderate oven for 2 hrs.
Porcelain on metal	• Wash with a sponge or cloth in warm, sudsy water or in the dishwasher (check manufacturer's instructions first). • Remove burned-on foods or stains by soaking the utensil or by using a non-abrasive cleansing powder and scrubber (such as a nylon net scrubber).
Copper	• Polish copper with various commercial copper cleaners. Or use a mixture of flour, salt, lemon juice and ammonia, or a mixture of flour and vinegar, to clean. After cleaning, wash in sudsy water, rinse and polish with a soft, clean cloth.
Tin	• Remove burned-on foods by boiling a solution of 1 qt. water and 2 tsp. baking soda in the utensil.

Cleaning Cookware and Utensils 🧹

Type of Material	How to Clean
Pewter	• Rub with a paste made from denatured alcohol and whiting, a fine abrasive powder available in hardware stores. • Let the paste dry on the metal, then wash, rinse and buff dry with a soft cloth
Silver	• Prepare a paste of whiting (an abrasive powder available in hardware stores) and household ammonia or alcohol. • Apply paste with a damp cloth, wash, rinse and wipe dry. • A soft brush, like a mascara brush, is helpful for cleaning small crevices.
Glass	• Wash in warm, sudsy water or in dishwasher. • To remove burned-on foods, pre-soak in sudsy water with a little baking soda added; scrub with non-abrasive scrubber. • To remove coffee and tea stains, soak in a solution of 2 tbsp. liquid chlorine bleach per 1 cup of water, or soak overnight in solution of 2 tbsp. automatic dishwasher detergent to 1 pot of warm water.
Non-stick finish	• Let the utensil cool after each use; then wash in hot, sudsy water, rinse and dry. Avoid abrasive cleansers or pads. After washing in dishwasher, wipe lightly with cooking oil. • To remove stains, simmer a mixture of 1 tbsp. liquid bleach, 1 tbsp. vinegar and 1 cup water for 5–10 min. in the utensil; wash, rinse and dry.

Sources: Metal Cookware Mfrs. Assn.; New York State Cooperative Extension.

🧹 General Cleaning Around the House

Type of Surface	How to Clean
Appliances (mixers, blenders, toasters, and so on)	• Clean outside surfaces with lukewarm, sudsy water; rinse and wipe dry with a soft cloth to remove water spots. • To protect the finish, use a creamy appliance wax occasionally. • Avoid using abrasive scouring pads or cleansers. Instead, soften any dried-on material with a sudsy, wet cloth or paper towel. • Some small electrical appliances can be immersed. Check instructions.
Stoves (gas and electric)	• Wait until range has cooled to wipe up food spills and spatters with a clean, damp, soft cloth or paper towel. • If food is baked on, try rubbing with a nylon net scrubber, which won't scratch the surface. • Clean the burner holes on a gas range with a small wire, paper clip or pipe cleaner. Never use toothpicks, which might break off and clog the holes. • If the burner heads or grates are hard to get clean, soak them in a mixture of 1 cup vinegar and 1 gallon hot water for 30 min.
Ovens (not self-cleaning)	• Leave ½ cup ammonia in the oven overnight (make sure the oven is cold). In the morning, mix the ammonia with 1 qt. warm water, and use it to clean the inside walls of the oven and oven door. • If necessary, use a mild scouring powder or steel wool to remove difficult spots. (Don't scour finished metals, glass or baked-on enamel; you should only scour porcelain enamel and stainless steel.) • Use commercial oven cleaners with caution, since they can damage the surface outside and around the oven.
Refrigerators	• Clean the inside with a solution of 1 tbsp. baking soda to 1 qt. warm water. Rinse with clean water and wipe dry. • Clean the folds in the gasket seal around the door with mild, sudsy water.

Type of Surface	How to Clean
Refrigerators (continued)	• Vacuum the condenser coils or fins on the bottom or at the back of the refrigerator to help keep the refrigerator running more efficiently. • Defrost the freezer when the frost is about ¼″ thick; if you wait longer, the freezer won't work as well. Turn the control to "off" or "defrost," and place pans of warm water in freezer compartment. Don't chip at frost with a sharp object. Wash the compartment with a baking-soda solution; rinse and wipe dry.
Wooden chopping surfaces	• Disinfect the surface occasionally with a mild bleach solution, rinse, and rub it with a thin coat of mineral or salad oil.
Plastic counter tops	• Wipe up dirt with a warm, sudsy solution. • To remove a stain, first try rubbing it with baking soda and a soft, damp cloth or sponge. If the stain persists, wipe with a little bleach spread on a cloth.
Sinks and tubs	• Clean most dirt with warm, sudsy water. Avoid coarse scouring powders, which scratch the surfaces. • Remove mild stains with baking soda. • To clean old sinks and tubs that are badly stained, try soaking them with vinegar or lemon juice. • For tougher stains, use a diluted solution of oxalic acid (1 part acid to 10 parts water). Oxalic acid is poisonous, so wear protective gloves. To apply oxalic acid solution to the vertical surface under a faucet, mix it with cornmeal, making a thick paste. Apply carefully to the stain; rinse off completely with water. Don't let any of it get on the chrome hardware.
Toilet bowls	• If you use commercial toilet-bowl cleaners, do not mix them with bleach or chlorinated cleansers: the combination can form poisonous gases. • Toilet bowls can also be cleaned with sudsy water or a mild cleanser. Be sure to clean under the inside rim of the bowl.

▨ General Cleaning Around the House

Type of Surface	How to Clean
Tile	• To remove soap spots or film from tile in the shower/bathtub area, wipe with a solution of water and a non-precipitating water softener, such as Calgon. • Try wiping the tiles with a vinegar solution (1 part vinegar to 4 parts water). Rinse with clear water and buff dry with a soft towel or cloth. • Clean the grout around the tile with a small, stiff brush; a toothbrush or a nail brush works well. If the grout is badly stained, scrub with a solution of chlorine bleach (¾ cup per 1 gallon of water).
Windows and mirrors	• Use a commercial cleaner or one of the following homemade solutions: either 1 qt. warm water and 1 tbsp. household ammonia, or 2 tbsp. vinegar and 1 qt. warm water. • Don't use soap since it may leave streaks, and don't wash windows in direct sunlight.
Walls and woodwork	• Dust surfaces first, to remove loose soil. • Wash or spot-clean *painted surfaces* with a solution of soap or mild detergent and water, or with a mild commercial household cleaner. If you use soap, soften the sudsy water and rinse water with 1 tbsp. borax per 1 qt. of water. • Do not use scouring powders, since they may remove the paint. • Wash walls from the bottom up (cleaning solution that runs down a dirty wall may cause streaks that are difficult to remove). Clean only a small area at a time; rinse with clear water and then go on to another spot overlapping the area. Dry with a soft cloth or towel. • Test the washability of a *wallcovering* in an inconspicuous place. If washable, use a mild detergent and cool water, and follow instructions above. • If wallcoverings are nonwashable, they can be cleaned by rubbing gently with art gum (a dough-type wallpaper cleaner), available in hardware stores.

General Cleaning Around the House 🔲

Type of Surface	How to Clean
Lampshades	• Dust with a clean, soft cloth or the dusting attachment of your vacuum cleaner. • *Fiberglass, plastic and other washable shades:* wipe with a clean, damp cloth. • *Silk, rayon, nylon and other washable shades that have been sewn to the frame and have colorfast trimmings:* dip them in a tub of mild, lukewarm suds; rinse in clean, lukewarm water. Dry quickly to prevent frames from rusting and staining fabric. Do not dry silk shades in direct sun; drying in front of a fan speeds up the process. • *Linen, cotton and hand-painted shades or shades with glued-on trim:* don't wash them in water. Use a dough-type wallpaper cleaner, available in hardware stores.
Venetian blinds	• Dust blinds regularly with dusting mitts or clean, absorbent gloves, or use a Venetian blind brush, which cleans several blinds at once. • Or tilt blinds flat and go over them with the dusting attachment of a vacuum cleaner. • Dip painted or plastic blinds in a tub of warm suds, or wash them individually after they've been removed from the tapes.
Window shades	• Clean washable shades by spreading them unrolled on a clean, flat surface and scrubbing with a brush or cloth wrung out in warm, sudsy water. Try not to wet the shade very much. Dry thoroughly before rerolling. • Clean nonwashable shades with art gum, cornmeal or a dough-type wallpaper cleaner.

Sources: U.S. Dept. of Agriculture, New York State Cooperative Extension Service.

▲ Cleaning Furniture

Type of Furniture	How to Clean
Bamboo, cane, wicker, reed	• Wash with a cloth or brush and sudsy water. If the furniture's very soiled, add a little ammonia to the sudsy water. Rinse with clean water and dry thoroughly.
Upholstered fabric	• Dust with your vacuum cleaner, a whisk broom or a coarse cloth. (If the cushions are down-filled—and aren't lined with down-proof ticking—they should be brushed, not vacuumed.) • Shampoo using detergent foam or suds to avoid wetting the furniture padding. Always test for shrinkage, fading or color bleeding on the back or in an inconspicuous area. Work quickly, a small area at a time. • To speed up drying, set furniture outdoors in the shade, indoors with windows open, or in front of an electric fan or heater. • To remove stains from fabrics, see procedures on pp. 4–6.
Upholstered leather	• Rub briskly with a lather made from warm water and castile or saddle soap. Wipe with a clean, damp cloth. Rub with a soft, dry cloth to restore sheen. • Do not use oils, furniture polishes or varnishes on leather—they may contain solvents that can make leather sticky.
Upholstered vinyl	• Sponge with warm water and a mild detergent solution. Allow the solution to soak a few minutes. Rub to loosen soil. Rinse with clear water and dry with a clean cloth or towel. • Do not use scouring powder, steel wool or strong household cleaners. • Use vinyl cleaners to remove grease and oily spots. • To remove other stains, try sponging the area with equal parts denatured alcohol and water, or with rubbing alcohol as it comes from the bottle; then apply saddle soap. Rinse with clear water and blot with a towel or soft cloth.

Type of Furniture	How to Clean
Wood	
Regular care	• Dust with a dry, lint-free cloth or the dust attachment of the vacuum cleaner. Add a few drops of furniture polish to the cloth, if you'd like, to help pick up dust. Move the cloth or the vacuum cleaner in the direction of the wood grain.
	• Water and liquids should never be allowed to stand on wooden surfaces; blot spills up quickly with a clean, dry cloth.
Waxing and polishing	• Because finishes vary, your best guide is to follow the manufacturer's directions. If they are not available, the advice below may be helpful, but be sure to test the products you use on an inconspicuous spot before proceeding.
	• *High luster or shine:* select a liquid polish or paste wax that indicates it will dry to a high shine.
	• *Low luster or satin finish:* select a greaseless cream polish or wax that protects the finish without increasing the shine.
	• *Natural oil finish:* re-oil occasionally with the type of oil used by the manufacturer, or rub with boiled linseed oil.
	• Once you have selected a product, do not switch back and forth.
	• Don't use waxes and polishes too frequently, as they may produce a film; this film can be removed by wiping the surface with a cloth dampened with mineral spirits or synthetic turpentine.
Removing spots, rings and candle wax	• To remove white spots or rings, sprinkle cigarette ashes, salt or rottenstone (available in hardware stores) over the spot. Rub gently in the direction of the wood grain with a cloth dipped in mineral or linseed oil. Wipe dry with a clean cloth. Repolish, wax or oil with the product you have been using.
	• To remove candle wax, scrape off as much as you can with your fingers, a soft kitchen scraper or a stick. Wipe any remaining spot with a cloth dipped in mineral oil or drycleaning fluid. Repolish, wax or oil.

Source: New York State Cooperative Extension Service.

▲ Caring for Your Floors

WASHING

Type of Surface	How to Clean
Linoleum, rubber, vinyl, stone, concrete, ceramic asphalt, marble	• Clean occasionally with a mop or cloth wrung out in water. A little mild detergent or household cleaner may be used. • Do not use harsh abrasives or strong alkaline cleaners. • Avoid wetting the floor too much, especially a floor with lots of seams.
Wood, cork	• Clean with a solvent such as turpentine, nontoxic drycleaning fluid, or a liquid- or paste-solvent cleaning wax. • Do not use water, unless otherwise directed by manufacturer of floor finish.

WAXING/FINISHING

Type of Surface	How to Wax/Finish
Linoleum, rubber, vinyl	• Use water-base waxes and finishes on any surface not damaged by water. Most are self-polishing. • To remove any wax build-up, follow the directions on the container or wipe with a solution of household ammonia and water (1 cup ammonia per 1 gallon of water).
Wood, cork	• Use spirit-solvent waxes, which are available in paste and liquid forms. Most need to be polished or buffed.

Source: New York State Cooperative Extension Service.

Type of Fiber	How to Wash	How to Dry
Cotton (whites)	• Use hot water; agitation is important, so don't overload the washer. • Use all-purpose soap or detergent. • Chlorine bleach may be necessary to remove stains. • Shrinkage is common unless item is pre-shrunk.	• Line drying is best to ensure the life of the fabric. • For machine drying, use normal settings; remove while still damp for ironing.
Cotton (light colors)	• Use warm water. Allow clothes to agitate freely. • Hotter water and chlorine bleach will remove soil more effectively, but may damage color. • Treat all pieces of an ensemble together so they'll continue to match. • Shrinkage is common unless item is pre-shrunk.	• Dry as above.
Cotton (dark colors)	• Use lukewarm water to avoid fading; then wash as above.	• Dry as above.
Linen	• Wash white and colored articles as suggested above. • Avoid heavy starches.	• Dry as above. • Ironing while damp is *very* important.

⚠ Washing and Drying Fabrics

Type of Fiber	How to Wash	How to Dry
Silk	• Dryclean or hand wash in warm water with a mild detergent promptly after wearing to prevent perspiration damage. • Choose an oxygen bleach if needed.	• Never use the dryer, which will cause yellowing. • Dry by rolling the article in an absorbent towel and then squeezing out the excess moisture. • Finish drying in normal room temperature air.
Wool	• Wash by hand or by machine with a mild detergent in cool water with some agitation (use a gentle cycle) or in warm water without agitation. • Dryclean to avoid shrinkage or *pilling* (formation of little balls of fiber on the surface of the article).	• Most woolens should not be dryer dried. • Roll the article in an absorbent towel, squeeze (*don't* wring) out excess moisture, and then pull the article into shape. • Allow it to finish drying on a flat surface in room temperature air. • Handle carefully when wet.
Nylon, acrylic, polyester	• Rub detergent on soiled spots before washing in warm water. Use gentle agitation. • Turn garments inside out to minimize pilling. • Put delicate items in a net bag when machine washing. • Wash white garments with other whites only. • Use chlorine bleach if fabrics are stained.	• Use the permanent press cycle, if your dryer has one. • Keep the load small so that items will tumble freely. • Keep them inside out to avoid pilling. • Remove clothes immediately after tumbling stops. Fold or hang right away.

Washing and Drying Fabrics ▥

Type of Fiber	How to Wash	How to Dry
Acetate, triacetate	• Drycleaning is recommended unless label indicates fabric is washable. • Pre-treat soiled places with detergent or soap. • Wash with a light-duty product. • Handle gently to avoid stretching; don't twist or wring garments.	• Dry at low temperature in machine or in normal room temperature air.
Rayon	• Hand wash delicate rayons in warm water. • Squeeze gently; do not twist or wring. • Heavier rayons can be washed in hot water with heavy-duty detergent.	• Drying for too long a time at too high a temperature may result in shrinkage and static electricity. • Remove from dryer while slightly damp and pull into shape.
Spandex	• Use warm water and detergent. • Avoid chlorine bleach.	• Dry at low temperature.
Rubber	• Wash often at low temperature to remove oily soils. • Avoid bleach.	• Dry at moderate temperature.
Blends	• A blend will take on the qualities of the fibers used in its production. Know what those combinations are. The best cleaning and drying guides are the labels or leaflets on care that most manufacturers attach to their merchandise.	

Sources: U.S. Dept. of Commerce, National Bureau of Standards; New York State Cooperative Extension Service; Association of Home Appliance Mfrs.

COOKING

📋 How to Save Money at the Supermarket

1. Shop with a purpose and with a list. Plan your menus for the entire week (or 2), and then organize your shopping list so that you have to pass through each section of the supermarket only once. If you have to return to the first aisle to pick up just one thing, you may find yourself attracted by other items.

2. Try to control your impulse buying. One study has estimated that almost 50% of purchases are entirely unplanned. Be especially careful at the start of your shopping trip, when your cart is nearly empty. You're more susceptible to high-priced, unplanned purchases then.

3. Get your shopping done within a half hour. Supermarkets are often very comfortable places to linger in, but one study suggests that customers spend at least 50 cents a minute after a half hour in the store.

4. Shop alone if you can. How many unplanned purchases are made when you've got "help"?

5. Never shop when you're hungry.

6. Use coupons wisely. Food companies often use coupon offers to promote either new products or old products that haven't been selling well. Ask yourself if you would have bought the item had there been no coupon, and compare prices with competing brands to see if you're really saving money.

7. Be a smart shopper. Be aware that grocery stores stock the highest-priced items at eye level. The lower-priced staples like flour, sugar and salt are often below eye level, as are bulk quantities of many items. Also be aware that foods displayed at the end of an aisle may appear to be on sale, but often are not.

8. Use unit pricing to find the brand and container-size of food that costs the least per pound, ounce or pint.

9. Avoid foods that are packaged as individual servings. Extra packaging usually boosts the price of the product.

10. When buying meat, consider the amount of lean meat in the cut, as well as the price per pound. A relatively high-priced cut with little or no waste may provide more meat for your money than a low-priced cut with a great deal of bone, gristle or fat. Chicken and turkey are often bargains compared to other meats, and fish is usually a good buy too.

11. Buy vegetables and fruits in season since they'll be at their peak of quality and their lowest price. Never buy the first crop; prices are sure to go down.

Sources: U.S. Dept. of Agriculture; Univ. of Vermont Extension Service; *Nutrition Action* (published by the Center for Science in the Public Interest; membership is available to the public for $20.00 per year).

Vegetable Buying and Storing Guide ⬒

Vegetable	What to Look for	Peak Season	Storage
Artichokes	Plump globes that are heavy in relation to size, with thick, tightly clinging, olive-green scales. *Avoid:* those with areas of brown on the scales.	April-May	Store in a plastic bag in the refrigerator; eat within 3–5 days.
Asparagus	Closed, compact tips with smooth, round spears. A rich green should cover most of the spear.	March-May	Store in the refrigerator (do not wash first); eat within 2–3 days.
Beans, Snap	Firm, crisp, slender pods with good green color.	April-Sept.	Store in the refrigerator; use within 1 week.
Beets	Firm, round, smooth beets with a deep red color. Wilted or decayed tops indicate a lack of freshness, but the roots may be satisfactory if firm.	All year	Remove the tops; store in the refrigerator; use within 2 weeks.
Broccoli	A firm, compact cluster of small flower buds. Color ranges from dark and sage green to purplish-green, depending on variety. *Avoid:* wilted or yellow leaves, thick stems and soft spots on the bud cluster.	All year	Store in the refrigerator; use within 3–5 days.
Brussels Sprouts	A fresh, bright-green color, tight-fitting outer leaves and firm body. *Avoid:* small holes or ragged leaves, which may indicate worm injury.	Oct.-Jan.	Store in the refrigerator; use within 3–5 days.
Cabbages (green cabbage, Savoy cabbage and red cabbage)	Firm or hard heads that are heavy for their size. Outer leaves should be a good green or red color (depending on type) and free from serious blemishes.	All year	Store in the refrigerator; use within 1–2 weeks.
Carrots	Firm, well-shaped roots with good orange color. *Avoid:* large green areas at top.	All year	Store in the refrigerator; use within 2 weeks.

▣ Vegetable Buying and Storing Guide

Vegetable	What to Look for	Peak Season	Storage
Cauliflower	White to creamy-white, compact, solid and clean curds (the white, edible portion). Size bears no relation to quality. Ignore small green leaflets extending through curd. *Avoid:* smudgy or speckled curd or many discolored spots.	Sept.-Jan.	Store in the refrigerator; use within 2 weeks.
Celery	Crisp, light- or medium-green stalks that are thick and solid with a glossy surface.	All year	Store in the refrigerator; use within 1 week.
Corn	Green husks, and ears that are covered with small, medium-yellow kernels. Stem ends (opposite from the silk) should not be too discolored or dried. Select corn that is cold to the touch.	May-Sept.	Store, unhusked and uncovered, in the refrigerator; use as soon as possible for sweetest flavor.
Cucumbers	Firm cucumbers of medium size with good green color. Good cucumbers typically have many small lumps on their surfaces and may also have some white or greenish-white color. *Avoid:* withered or shriveled ends.	All year	Wash, dry and store in the refrigerator; use within 1 week.
Eggplants	Firm, heavy, smooth eggplants with uniformly dark purple to purple-black skin. *Avoid:* those with irregular dark brown spots.	All year	Store at cool room temperature (around 60° F.). Temperature below 50° F. may cause chilling injury.
Endive, Escarole and Chicory	Cold, crisp, green leavs. *Avoid:* reddish discoloration of the hearts.	All year	Wash, drain and store in the refrigerator; use within 1 week.
Garlic	Firm, plump bulbs with clean, dry, unbroken skins.	All year	Store open in a cool, dry place; do not refrigerate; use within 1 month.

Vegetable Buying and Storing Guide 🗄

Vegetable	What to Look for	Peak Season	Storage
Greens (spinach, kale, collards, chard)	Crisp, green leaves. *Avoid:* coarse stems or soft, yellowing leaves.	All year	Wash in cold water, drain well, store in plastic bags or crisper in refrigerator; use within 3–5 days.
Lettuce *Iceberg*	Large, round and solid heads that "give" slightly when squeezed. Outer leaves should be medium-green; inner leaves are lighter in color.	All year	Remove core and rinse end up under cold, running water. Drain thoroughly. Store in a tightly closed plastic bag.
Boston and bibb	Smaller head with light-green leaves.	All year	Wash and drain well. Store in crisper or plastic bag in fridge. Use within 3–5 days.
Romaine	Crisp, dark-green leaves in loosely folded head.	All year	As above.
Leaf	Broad, loose and fairly smooth leaves that vary in color with variety.	All year	As above.
Mushrooms	Small to medium mushrooms with white, cream-colored or tan caps. Caps should either be closed around the stem or moderately open with pink or light-tan gills.	All year	Store in the crisper in a paper bag or covered with a damp paper towel. Use within 5 days.
Okra	Tender, bright-green pods (the tips will bend with very slight pressure) 2–4½" long.	May-Sept.	Store in a plastic bag in the refrigerator; use within 3–5 days.
Onions (dry)	Hard or firm globes with dry, crackly skins and small necks. *Avoid:* green spots: wet, soggy necks; sprouts.	All year	Store at room temperature, or slightly cooler, in loosely woven or open-mesh containers; will keep for several months.

▢ Vegetable Buying and Storing Guide

Vegetable	What to Look for	Peak Season	Storage
Onions (green) *Scallions Leeks*	Bunches with crisp, green tops and white portions extending 2–3″ up from the bulb end.	All year	Store in a plastic bag in the refrigerator; use within 3–5 days.
Parsley	Crisp, bright-green leaves.	All year	Store in a plastic bag in the refrigerator; use within 3–5 days.
Parsnips, Turnips	Smooth, firm, well-shaped roots of small to medium width.	May-Sept.	Remove tops; store in plastic bags in the refrigerator; use within 2 weeks.
Peppers (sweet bell, red, chili)	Firm peppers with relatively heavy weight, glossy sheen and bright-green color (which may be tinged with red). *Avoid:* soft, watery spots on sides and thin walls.	All year	Wash, dry and store in the crisper or in plastic bags in the refrigerator; use within 1 week.
Potatoes *New* (best used for boiling or creaming) *General purpose* (used for boiling, frying and baking) *Baking*	Firm, well-shaped, reasonably smooth potatoes. *Avoid:* green discoloration and sprouts.	All year	Never refrigerate; store in a dark, dry place with good ventilation, with a temperature of about 45–50° ₊. Will keep, in this manner, for months.
Radishes	Plump, round, firm, medium-size (¾–1⅛″ in diameter) radishes with good red color. *Avoid:* very large radishes or those with yellow tops.	All year	Remove tops; store in a plastic bag in the refrigerator; use within 2 weeks.

Vegetable Buying and Storing Guide ☐

Vegetable	What to Look for	Peak Season	Storage
Rutabagas	Firm, smooth, round or moderately elongated rutabagas with relatively heavy weight for their size. Size is not important. *Avoid:* deep cuts or punctures.	May-Oct.	Store at cool room temperature (around 60° F.); will keep for several months.
Squash (summer) **Crookneck Straightneck Patty pan Zucchini**	Small to medium, well-developed, firm squash with a glossy skin. *Avoid:* dull, tough surface.	May-Sept.	Store in crisper or plastic bags in the refrigerator; use within 5–8 days.
Squash (winter) **Acorn Butternut Hubbard Delicious Banana Buttercup**	Hard, tough rind; heavy weight for its size. Slight variations in skin color are not important. *Avoid:* soft areas, sunburnt spots, or cuts.	Sept.-Feb.	Don't refrigerate; store at cool room temperature (around 60° F.); will keep for several months.
Sweet Potatoes	Thick, medium-sized, firm sweet potatoes with smooth, bright, uniformly colored skins. *Avoid:* any cuts or blemishes.	Sept.-April	Don't refrigerate; store at cool room temperature (around 60° F.); will keep for several months. Handle gently to avoid bruising.
Tomatoes	Smooth, firm and plump tomatoes with an overall rich, red color. *Avoid:* green or yellow areas or cracks near the stem scar as well as soft, water-soaked spots or depressed areas.	All year	Store ripe tomatoes in a cool, dark place and use as soon as possible. Keep unripe tomatoes at room temperature away from direct sunlight until they ripen. Putting them in a brown paper bag hastens ripening.

Sources: U.S. Dept. of Agriculture; Lunds, Inc., Minneapolis.

▢ Fruit Buying and Storing Guide

Fruit	What to Look for	Peak Season	Ripening/ Storage
Apples	Firm, crisp fruit with good color for the variety. *Avoid:* discoloration, shriveling, apples that yield to slight pressure on the skin.	All year, depending on the variety (see pp. 39–40)	Keep in refrigerator or cool, dark place. Use ripe fruit within 1 week.
Apricots	Plump, well-formed, fairly firm fruit with deep-yellow or yellowish-orange color.	June-July	Store in paper bag in a warm room to ripen. Then keep in refrigerator for 3–5 days.
Avocado	Color ranging from purple-black to green, depending on variety. Irregular brown marks on the surface do not affect quality. *Avoid:* dark, sunken spots or cracked surfaces.	All year	Hold at room temperature for a few days to ripen. Ripe when flesh is slightly soft and yields to gentle pressure. Refrigerate ripe fruit and use as soon as possible.
Bananas	Firm, plump fruit. Color ranges from green to brown: best-eating quality is reached when the skin is solid yellow specked with brown. *Avoid:* grayish-yellow or bruised fruit.	All year	Ripen at 70° F. room temperature; when at stage of preferred ripeness, refrigerate and use as soon as possible.
Blueberries	Plump, firm, dry berries. Color should be dark blue with a silvery bloom. *Avoid:* baskets showing signs of bruised or leaking fruit.	May-Sept.	Pack loosely, cover and refrigerate immediately. Use as soon as possible.
Cantaloupe	Yellowish cast to the rind, with veining that is thick and coarse. Fruit should have no stem and should give slightly at the blossom end when pressed gently. Ripe cantaloupes have a pleasant odor. *Avoid:* a pronounced yellow rind color, large bruises and a softening over the entire rind.	May-Sept.	Hold at room temperature for a few days to ripen; then refrigerate and use as soon as possible.

Fruit Buying and Storing Guide ▢

Vegetable	What to Look for	Peak Season	Storage
Casaba Melon	Golden-yellow rind with a slight softening at the blossom end. They have no odor. *Avoid:* dark, water-soaked spots.	July-Nov.	Hold at room temperature for a few days to ripen; then refrigerate and use as soon as possible.
Cherries	Plump, glossy fruit with dark color ranging from deep red to black. Firm but not hard. *Avoid:* dried stems, shrivelling, and leaking flesh.	May-Aug.	Will ripen at room temperature. Refrigerate ripe fruit immediately and use within 2 days.
Cranberries	Plump, firm, red to reddish-black berries.	Sept.-Jan.	Refrigerate and use within 1½ weeks. For longer storage, freeze in original package.
Crenshaw Melon	Deep golden-yellow rind that yields slightly to thumb pressure. Pleasant odor when ripe. *Avoid:* sunken, water-soaked spots.	Aug.-Sept.	Hold at room temperature for a few days to ripen; then refrigerate and use as soon as possible.
Grapefruit	Firm, thick-skinned, globular fruit that is heavy for its size. Skin defects—green tinge, scars, etc.—do not affect quality. *Avoid:* soft, discolored areas on peel at stem end; loose or wrinkled skin.	Jan.-May	Refrigerate or leave at room temperature. Use within 2 weeks.
Grapes	Plump, firm grapes that are securely attached to green, pliable stems. Green grapes are sweetest when yellowish-green in color. *Avoid:* wrinkled or leaking berries, grapes with bleached areas around stem.	July-Nov.	Grapes are usually ripe when shipped to market but will ripen further at room temperature. Refrigerate ripe fruit immediately and use as soon as possible.

⬚ Fruit Buying and Storing Guide

Fruit	What to Look for	Peak Season	Ripening/ Storage
Honeydew Melon	Creamy or yellowish-white rind with a velvety or waxy feel, distinctive melon aroma. *Avoid:* dead-white or greenish-white color and hard, smooth rind.	June-Oct.	Hold at room temperature to ripen; then refrigerate and use as soon as possible.
Lemons	Fruit that is heavy for its size with fairly smooth-textured skin. *Avoid:* shrivelled skin, soft spots.	All year	Keep at room temperature or refrigerate. Use within 2 weeks.
Limes	Fruit heavy for its size with bright-green, glossy skin. *Avoid:* dull, dry skin.	All year	Keep at room temperature or refrigerate. Use within 2 weeks.
Mangos	Green skin with yellowish to red areas (these increase with ripeness). *Avoid:* grayish skin discoloration, pitting or black spots.	May-Aug.	Keep at room temperature until very soft. Then refrigerate and use as soon as possible.
Nectarines	Orange-yellow color between red areas, slight softening of the fruit around the stem end. *Avoid:* hard, dull or shrivelled fruit.	June-Sept.	Hold at room temperature to ripen; then refrigerate and use within 3–5 days.
Oranges	Firm and heavy oranges with finely textured skin. Green skin color or russeting (brown or black mottling or speckling over skin) does not affect quality. *Avoid:* very rough or dull, dry skin; soft spots.	All year	Store at room temperature or refrigerate. Use within 2 weeks.
Papayas	Medium, well-sized fruit that is at least half yellow.	May-June; Oct.-Dec.	Ripen at room temperature until skin is primarily golden; then refrigerate and use as soon as possible.

Fruit Buying and Storing Guide ⬚

Fruit	What to Look for	Peak Season	Ripening/ Storage
Peaches	Fairly firm or slightly soft fruit with a yellowish or cream-colored background skin color (between red patches). *Avoid:* green, hard peaches or those with large bruises.	June-Sept.	Hold at room temperature to soften; then refrigerate promptly and use within 3–5 days.
Pears	Fairly firm fruit. *Bartletts:* pale to rich yellow color; *Anjou/Comice:* light to yellowish green; *Bosc:* greenish to brownish yellow. Russeting (brown speckling) does not affect quality. *Avoid:* shriveled fruit with dull skin and slight weakening of the flesh near the stem.	*Bartlett:* Aug.-Nov.; *Anjou, Bosc, Comice:* Nov.-May	Hold at room temperature in a closed paper bag until stem end yields to pressure; then refrigerate and use within 3–5 days.
Persian Melon	Yellowish cast to the rind and veining that is thick and coarse. Fruit should have no stem and should give slightly at the blossom end when pressed gently.	Aug.-Sept.	Hold at room temperature until ripe; then refrigerate and use as soon as possible.
Persimmons	Plump, smooth, highly colored fruit with a green cap.	Oct.-Dec.	Keep at room temperature until soft; then refrigerate and use as soon as possible.
Pineapples	Plump, glossy eyes or pips; firmness; a lively color (golden-yellow, orange-yellow or reddish-brown depending on the variety); leaves or spikes that pull out easily; fruit that is heavy for its size; a rich, sweet smell. *Avoid:* watery or dark eyes; dull, yellowish-green color.	April-May	Ripen at room temperature (normally within 3 days). Then refrigerate and use as soon as possible. Ripen and store crown-side down.
Plums	Good color for the variety with fairly firm to slightly soft flesh. *Avoid:* skin breaks; brownish discoloration; hard, shriveled or leaking fruit.	June-Sept.	Hold at room temperature until flesh yields to pressure; then refrigerate and use within 3–5 days.

📖 Fruit Buying and Storing Guide

Fruit	What to Look for	Peak Season	Ripening/ Storage
Pomegranates	Pink or bright red rind. *Avoid:* dry-looking fruits.	Sept.-Nov.	Keep cold and humid.
Prunes	(Same as plums)	Aug.-Oct.	(Same as plums)
Raspberries (blackberries, dewberries, loganberries, youngberries)	Bright, clean berries with uniform good color. *Avoid:* those with attached stem caps, leaky or moldy berries (look for stained spots on containers).	June-Aug.	Refrigerate immediately and use as soon as possible.
Rhubarb	Firm, bright stems with large amounts of pink or red color. *Avoid:* very slender or very thick stems, wilted stalks.	Jan.-July	Store in refrigerator; use within 3–5 days.
Strawberries	Firm, dry, full-red berries with bright luster and green caps still attached. *Avoid:* berries with large seedy areas, a shrunken appearance or mold.	April-June	Refrigerate immediately, unwashed, with caps intact; hull and wash just before using.
Tangerines	Deep yellow or orange color, fruit that is heavy for its size. A puffy appearance and feel are normal. *Avoid:* cut skin or soft spots.	Dec.-Jan.	Refrigerate and use as soon as possible.
Watermelon	*Whole:* firm, smooth melons with a dullness on the rind. Underside should be yellowish or cream-white; ends of melon should be filled out. *Avoid:* stark-white or greenish-colored undersides. *Cut:* firm, red, juicy flesh with black seeds. *Avoid:* white streaks in flesh, whiteish seeds.	June-Aug.	Keep at room temperature or refrigerate; use within 3–5 days.

Sources: U.S. Dept. of Agriculture; Lunds, Inc., Minneapolis.

Variety	When in Season	What They're Like	Where to Use		
			Raw	General Cooking	Baking Whole
Beacon	Aug.-Sept.	Medium; red; mild.		●	●
Cortland	Sept.-Feb.	Medium to large; bright red with stripes; juicy, slightly tart, tender, crisp, fragrant.	●	●	●
Golden Delicious	Sept.-June	Medium to large; yellow; sweet, semi-firm, crisp.	●	●	●
Granny Smith	Nov.-June	Medium to large; bright green; moderately tart, juicy, crisp.	●	●	●
Gravenstein	Aug.-Oct.	Medium; yellow; firm, tart, juicy, spicy.	●	●	
Greening	Oct.-April	Large; green or yellow; firm, crisp.		●	●
Haralson	Oct.-March	Medium, red; tart, juicy.	●	●	●
Jonathan	Sept.-April	Small to medium; deep red; juicy, moderately tart, tender, crisp, fragrant.	●	●	●
McIntosh	Sept.-April	Medium to large; bright dark red with stripes; juicy, slightly tart, tender, crisp, fragrant.	●	●	●
Newtown Pippin	Sept.-May	Small to medium; yellow-green; firm, mildly tart.	●	●	●
Prairie Spy	Oct.-April	Medium to large; bright red with stripes; very juicy, moderately tart, tender, crisp, fragrant.	●	●	●
Red Delicious	Sept.-June	Medium to large; deep red; 5 knobs on blossom end; sweet, tender, fragrant.	●		
Rome Beauty	Oct.-July	Large; yellow mingled with red; juicy, slightly tart, firm, crisp.	●	●	●
Spartan	Oct.-May	Medium; deep red; firm, crisp, juicy.	●	●	

🗂 Apple Buying Guide

Variety	When in Season	What They're Like	Where to Use		
			Raw	General Cooking	Baking Whole
Staymen	Oct.-June	Medium to large; dull red with stripes; juicy, tart. semifirm, crisp.	●	●	●
Wealthy	Sept.-Nov.	Medium; striped red; crisp, juicy.	●	●	
Winesap	Oct.-Sept.	Small to medium; deep bright red with small scattered white dots; very juicy, slightly tart, firm, crisp, fragrant.	●	●	●
Yellow Newton	Sept.-June	Medium; yellow; juicy, moderately tart.	●	●	
York Imperial	Oct.-June	Medium to large; light or purplish red over yellow; usually lopsided in shape; slightly tart, firm, crisp.		●	●

Sources: U.S. Dept. of Agriculture.

All About Beans, Peas and Lentils ☐

Storing

- After packages are opened, dry beans, peas and lentils should be stored in tightly covered containers and kept in a cool, dry place.
- Cooked beans should be tightly covered and stored in the refrigerator; use within a day or two.

Soaking

- Dry beans and whole peas should be soaked before cooking; lentils and split peas used in soups may be cooked without soaking.
- Always wash beans thoroughly before soaking.
- *Traditional method.* To 1 lb. (1½–2 cups) of dry beans or peas, add 6 cups cold water and 1½ tsp. salt. Let stand overnight or for 6–8 hrs. Drain and rinse before cooking.
- *Quick method.* To 1 lb. (1½–2 cups) of dry beans or peas, add 6–8 cups hot water with or without 1½ tsp. salt. Heat; let boil 3 min.; cover and set aside for 1 hr. Drain, rinse and cool before cooking.
- Be sure that whatever pot you use to soak the beans or peas in is large enough to allow them to expand 2½ times.

Cooking

- *Standard method.* Put soaked beans, peas or lentils into a good-sized kettle. If you start with 1 lb. (1½–2 cups) of dried beans, add 6 cups hot water (or to about 1 in. above the beans). Add 2 tsp. oil or butter and 2 tsp. salt. Simmer gently until they are done (generally 1½–2 hrs.).
- *Savory method.* Follow directions above, but use 2 tsp. onion salt and ¼ tsp. garlic salt instead of plain salt. Add 1 tbsp. chicken stock, or 3–4 bouillon cubes, and ¼ tsp. white pepper.

Yield

- 1 lb. = 1½ cups, dry = 5–6 cups, cooked.

Sources: U.S. Dept. of Agriculture, California Dry Bean Advisory Board.

⬚ All About Rice and Pasta

RICE

Cooking	• *Top-of-the-range method.* In a 2- or 3-quart saucepan, combine 1 cup uncooked rice with 2 cups liquid (2½ cups for brown rice), 1 tbsp. butter and 1 tsp. salt. Bring the ingredients to a boil and stir once or twice. Lower heat to simmer and cover pan tightly. Cook for 15 min. (45 min. for brown rice) or until rice is tender and liquid is absorbed. • *Oven method.* In a baking dish, combine 1 cup uncooked rice with 2 cups boiling liquid (2½ cups for brown rice), 1 tbsp. butter and 1 tsp. salt. Cover dish tightly and bake at 350°F. for 25–30 min. (1 hr. for brown rice).
Tips	• For drier rice, use 2 tbsp. less liquid; or, after cooking, fluff rice with fork and let stand, covered, for 5–10 min. • When reheating rice, add 2 tbsp. liquid for each cup. Cover; heat for 5 min.
Yield	• 1 cup uncooked, white or brown = 3–4 cups, cooked.

Source: Rice Council of America.

PASTA

Cooking	• To 3 qts. rapidly boiling water, gradually add 8 oz. pasta along with 2 tsp. salt. Make sure water continues to boil as you add pasta. Cook, uncovered, stirring occasionally. Don't overcook. Cook "al dente" (tender to the tooth)—5–10 min. is generally enough. Drain in colander. Rinse only when making salads.
Tips	• To keep pasta from sticking together, add 1 tbsp. olive oil to cooking water. • 1 lb. of pasta requires 4–6 qts. of water for cooking.
Yield	• 1 lb. uncooked spaghetti = 6½ cups, cooked.

Source: National Pasta Assn.

Storing

- Nuts will keep in the shell at room temperature for short periods of time; for prolonged storage, keep them in a cool, dry place.
- Shelled nuts will keep fresh for several months when refrigerated in tightly closed containers.
- Shelled or unshelled nuts will keep for up to a year when frozen in tightly closed containers.

Removing skins

- *Blanching* is the best method for almonds, peanuts and chestnuts. Place nuts in boiling water and let stand 2–3 min. Drain. Slide skin off with your fingers. Spread nuts on absorbent paper to dry.
- *Roasting* is the best method for filberts. Spread nuts in single layer in shallow baking pan. Bake at 300° F. for 10–15 min. or until heated through; stir occasionally. Cool slightly, and slip skins off with your fingers.

Roasting or toasting

- To roast, spread nuts on baking sheet and heat in oven for 5–15 min. at 350° F. or until lightly browned; stir occasionally.
- To toast, heat nutmeats slowly on top of range for 10–15 min. or until lightly browned; stir occasionally.
- Nuts continue to brown slightly after being removed from heat, so avoid overbrowning.

Yields

- 1 lb. unshelled nuts will yield the following amounts (by weight and volume) of shelled nuts:

	Oz.	Cups
Almonds, whole	6⅓	1¼
Brazil nuts, whole	7⅔	1½
Filberts, whole	7⅓	1½
Peanuts, roasted	11⅔	2¼
Pecans, halved	8½	2¼
Walnuts, chopped	3½	¾
Walnuts, halved	7¼	2

Source: U.S. Dept. of Agriculture.

🗄 Safe Food Storage Guide

Food	Refrigerator (at 35–40° F.)	Freezer (at 0° F.)
Fresh meats		
Roasts (beef)	3–5 days	6–12 months
Roasts (pork, veal and lamb)	3–5 days	4–8 months
Steaks (beef)	3–5 days	6–12 months
Chops (lamb)	3–5 days	6–9 months
Chops (pork)	3–5 days	3–4 months
Ground and stew meats	1–2 days	3–4 months
Variety meats (liver, kidney, etc.)	1–2 days	3–4 months
Sausage (pork)	1–2 days	1–2 months
Processed meats		
Bacon	1 week	1 month
Hot dogs	1 week	2 weeks
Ham (whole)	1 week	1–2 months
Ham (half)	5 days	1–2 months
Ham (slices)	3 days	1–2 weeks
Luncheon meats	3–5 days	2 weeks
Sausage (smoked)	1 week	2 weeks
Cooked meats		
Cooked meat and meat dishes	3–4 days	2–3 months
Gravy and meat broth	1–2 days	2–3 months
Fresh poultry		
Chicken and turkey (whole)	1–2 days	12 months
Chicken (pieces)	1–2 days	9 months
Turkey (pieces)	1–2 days	6 months
Duck and goose (whole)	1–2 days	6 months
Giblets	1–2 days	3 months
Cooked poultry		
Pieces (covered with broth)	1–2 days	6 months
Pieces (not covered)	1–2 days	1 month
Cooked poultry dishes	1–2 days	6 months
Fried chicken	1–2 days	4 months

Safe Food Storage Guide 🗄

Food	Refrigerator (at 35–40° F.)	Freezer (at 0° F.)
Fresh fish	1–2 days	6–9 months
Commercially frozen fish		
Shrimp and fillets of lean fish	—	3–4 months
Clams (shucked) and cooked fish	—	3 months
Fillets of fatty fish and crab meat	—	2–3 months
Oysters (shucked)	—	1 month
Fresh fruits and vegetables	1 day – 2 weeks (for details, see charts, pp. 29 – 40)	—
Frozen fruits and vegetables	—	8–12 months
Dairy products		
Milk (whole, skim, 2%)	1 week	—
Cream	1 week	—
Ice cream and other frozen desserts	—	1 month
Cottage cheese	1 week	—
Hard cheeses (like cheddar)	1–2 months	6 months
Soft cheeses (like Brie or cream)	2 weeks	1 month
Cheese spreads	1–2 weeks	—
Butter, margarine	2 weeks	2 months
Eggs (in shell)	1 week	—
Prepared foods		
Breads	5–7 days	2–3 months
Cakes, custard pies	1–2 days	4–9 months
Fruit pies	3–4 days	3–6 months

Source: U.S. Dept. of Agriculture.

☐ Food Substitutions Chart

Food	If You're Out of This Amount:	Use This:
Baking powder, double-acting	1 tsp.	¼ tsp. baking soda plus ½ cup buttermilk (and reduce liquid by ½ cup)
Butter	1 cup	⅞–1 cup lard or shortening plus ½ tsp. salt
Buttermilk, for baking	1 cup	1 cup whole milk plus 1 tbsp. vinegar or lemon juice
Catsup	1 cup	1 8-oz. can tomato sauce plus ½ cup brown sugar and 2 tbsp. vinegar
Chocolate, unsweetened	1 square	3–4 tbsp. cocoa plus 1 tbsp. shortening
Cornstarch	1 tbsp.	2 tbsp. all-purpose flour
Corn syrup	1 cup	1¼ cups sugar plus ¼ cup liquid
Cream, heavy	1 cup	¾ cup milk plus ⅓ cup butter
Eggs	2 egg yolks	1 whole egg
Flour, for thickening	1 tbsp.	½ tbsp. cornstarch
Garlic	1 clove	⅛ tsp. garlic powder
Honey	1 cup	1¼ cups sugar plus ¼ cup liquid

Food Substitutions Chart 🔲

Food	If You're Out of This Amount:	Use This:
Milk	1 cup, whole	½ cup evaporated milk plus ½ cup water
Onion	1 cup, chopped	1 tbsp. instant minced (rehydrated)
Sour cream, for cooking	1 cup	1 tbsp. lemon juice added to enough evaporated milk to make a cup
Tomato sauce	2 cups	¾ cup tomato paste plus 1 cup water
Yogurt	1 cup	1 cup buttermilk

Food Equivalents Chart 🔲

Food	This Amount:	Equals This:
Almonds, whole	1 lb.	1¼ cups
Apples	1 lb. 3 lbs.	3 medium 8 cups, sliced
Bananas	1 lb. (3–4)	2 cups, mashed
Beans Kidney, dry Lima, dry Navy, dry	 1 lb. (1½–2 cups) 1 lb. 1½–2 cups) 1 lb. (1½–2 cups)	 5–6 cups, cooked 5–6 cups, cooked 5–6 cups, cooked
Bread	1 slice, toasted or dried 1 lb. loaf	⅓ cup, crumbs 10 cups, small bread cubes
Butter, margarine	1 oz. 1 stick 1 lb.	2 tbsp. ½ cup 2 cups

⊟ Food Equivalents Chart

Food	This Amount:	Equals This:
Cabbage	1 lb.	3½–4½ cups raw, shredded (or 2 cups, cooked)
Carrots	1 lb.	3 cups, shredded
Celery	1 stalk	⅓ cup, diced
Cheese	¼ lb.	1 cup, shredded
Chocolate	1 square	1 oz.
Cottage cheese	1 lb.	2 cups
Cream, heavy	1 cup	2 cups, whipped
Dates	1 lb.	2½ cups, pitted
Eggs	4–6 whole 8–10 whites 10–14 yolks	1 cup 1 cup 1 cup
Figs	1 lb.	2⅔ cups, chopped
Flour Cake White Whole wheat	 1 cup minus 2 tbsp. 1 lb. 1 cup plus 2 tbsp. 1 lb. 1 lb.	 1 cup, sifted 4½ cups, sifted 1 cup, sifted 4 cups, sifted 3½ cups
Green pepper	1 large	1 cup, diced
Honey	1 lb.	1⅓ cups
Lemon	1 medium	2–3 tbsp. juice; 2 tsp. rind
Mushrooms	½ lb., fresh 6 oz., canned	2½ cups, sliced 1 lb. fresh
Noodles	4 oz.	2–2½ cups, cooked

Food Equivalents Chart

Food	This Amount:	Equals This:
Onions	1 medium	½ cup, chopped
Peaches	4 medium	2 cups, peeled and sliced
Peanuts	1 lb., shelled	2¼ cups
Pecans, halved	1 lb.	2¼ cups
Potatoes	1 lb. (3 medium)	2 cups, cooked and mashed
Prunes	1 lb.	2¼ cups, pitted
Raisins	1 lb.	2¾ cups
Rice	1 lb. 1 cup, uncooked	2–2½ cups, uncooked 3–4 cups, cooked
Spaghetti	1 lb.	6½ cups, cooked
Sugar Brown (firmly packed) Granulated Powdered	 1 lb. 1 lb. 1 lb.	 2¼ cups 2 cups 3½ cups
Tomatoes	1 lb. 1 8–oz. can 1 8–8 oz. can	3–4 small 1 lb. fresh 1 cup
Walnuts, chopped	1 lb.	¾ cup
Yeast, dry	1 pkg.	1 tbsp.

How to Estimate Servings Needed

Food	Servings per Unit
Meat	
Much bone or gristle	1 or 2 per lb.
Medium amounts of bone	2 or 3 per lb.
Little or no bone	3 or 4 per lb.
Poultry	
Chicken	2 or 3 per lb.
Turkey	2 or 3 per lb.
Duck and goose	2 per lb.
Fish	
Whole	1 or 2 per lb.
Dressed or pan-dressed	2 or 3 per lb.
Portions or steaks	3 per lb.
Fillets	3 or 4 per lb.
Clams	2 per dozen
Crabs	1–2 per lb.
Lobsters	1 per lb.
Oysters	2 per dozen
Scallops	3 per lb.
Shrimp	3 per lb.
Fresh vegetables	
Asparagus	3 or 4 per lb.
Beans, green	5 or 6 per lb.
Beans, lima	2 per lb.
Beets, diced	3 or 4 per lb.
Broccoli	3 or 4 per lb.
Brussel sprouts	4 or 5 per lb.
Cabbage	
Raw, shredded	9 or 10 per lb.
Cooked	4 or 5 per lb.
Carrots	
Raw, diced or shredded	5 or 6 per lb.
Cooked	4 per lb.
Cauliflower	3 per lb.
Celery	
Raw, chopped or diced	5 or 6 per lb.
Cooked	4 per lb.
Kale	5 or 6 per lb.
Okra	4 or 5 per lb.

Food	Servings per Unit
Onions, cooked	3 or 4 per lb.
Parsnips	4 per lb.
Peas	2 per lb.
Potatoes	4 per lb.
Spinach	4 per lb.
Squash, summer	3 or 4 per lb.
Squash, winter	2 or 3 per lb.
Sweet potatoes	3 or 4 per lb.
Tomatoes, raw, sliced or diced	4 per lb.
Frozen vegetables	
Asparagus	2 or 3 per pkg. (9–10 oz.)
Beans, green	3 or 4 per pkg. (9–10 oz.)
Beans, lima	3 or 4 per pkg. (9–10 oz.)
Broccoli	3 per pkg. (9–10 oz.)
Brussel sprouts	3 per pkg. (9–10 oz.)
Cauliflower	3 per pkg. (9–10 oz.)
Corn, whole kernel	3 per pkg. (9–10 oz.)
Kale	2 or 3 per pkg. (9–10 oz.)
Peas	3 per pkg. (9–10 oz.)
Spinach	2 or 3 per pkg. (9–10 oz.)
Canned vegetables	
Most vegetables	3 or 4 per 16-oz. can
Greens, such as kale or spinach	2 or 3 per 16-oz. can
Fresh fruit	
Apples, bananas, peaches, pears, plums	3 or 4 per lb.
Apricots, cherries, grapes	5 or 6 per lb.
Blueberries, raspberries	4 or 5 per pt.
Strawberries	8 or 9 per qt.
Frozen fruit	
Blueberries	3 or 4 per pkg. (10–12 oz.)
Peaches	2 or 3 per pkg. (10–12 oz.)
Raspberries	2 or 3 per pkg. (10–12 oz.)
Strawberries	2 or 3 per pkg. (10–12 oz.)
Canned fruit	
Served with liquid	4 per 16-oz. can
Drained	2 or 3 per 16-oz. can

Source: U.S. Dept. of Agriculture.

Cooking Measurements

Equivalents

Unit	Tsp.	Tbsp.	Fluid Ounce	Cup	Pint	Quart	Gallon
1 tsp.	1	1/3	1/6	—	—	—	—
1 tbsp.	3	1	1/2	1/16	1/32	—	—
1 fluid ounce	6	2	1	1/8	1/16	1/32	—
1 cup	48	16	8	1	1/2	1/4	1/16
1 pint	—	—	16	2	1	1/2	1/8
1 quart	—	—	32	4	2	1	1/4
1 gallon	—	—	—	16	8	4	1

Miscellaneous Measurements

1 jigger = 3 tablespoons (1½ fluid ounces)
1 dash = 6–7 drops (less than 1/8 teaspoon)
8 (dry) quarts = 1 peck
4 pecks = 1 bushel
16 (dry) ounces = 1 pound

Cooking Temperatures

Heat	Temp. (Fahrenheit)
Very slow	250–275°
Slow	300–325°
Moderate	350–375°
Hot	400–425°
Very hot	450–475°
Broil	500–525°

Can Sizes

Can Sizes	Approximate Cups
8 oz.	1
Picnic	1¼
No. 300	1¾
No. 303	2
No. 2	2½
No. 2½	3½

🗂 5 Ways to Cook Meat

1. Roast
- Season with salt and pepper.
- Place meat fat side up on rack in open roasting pan.
- Insert meat thermometer into roast so that tip is in center but not touching bone or fat.
- Do not add water. Do not cover. Do not baste.
- Roast in slow oven (300–325° F.).
- Roast to desired degree of doneness. (See chart, pp. 53–54.)

2. Broil
- Set oven regulator for broiling. Preheat broiler, if desired.
- Broil meat 2–5″ from heat.
- Broil until top of meat is brown.

- Season with salt and pepper.
- Turn meat and cook until done. (See chart, p. 56.)
- Season and serve at once.

3. Panboil
- Place meat in heavy frying pan.
- Do not add fat or water. Do not cover.
- Cook slowly, turning occasionally.
- Pour fat from pan as it accumulates.
- Brown meat on all sides.
- Season and serve at once.

4. Panfry
- Brown meat on both sides in small amount of fat.
- Season with salt and pepper.

- Do not cover.
- Cook at moderate temperature until done, stirring occasionally.
- Remove from pan and serve at once.

5. Braise
- Brown meat on all sides in fat in heavy utensil.
- Season with salt and pepper.
- Add small amount of liquid.
- Cover tightly.
- Cook at low temperature until tender. (See chart, p. 57.)

Source: National Live Stock and Meat Board.

Kind of Meat	Ready-to-Cook Weight	Oven Temp.	Cooking Time (Min. per Lb.)	Internal Temp. of Meat When Done
Beef				
Standing rib roast	6–8 lbs.	300–325° F.	23–25	140° F. (rare)
	6–8 lbs.	300–325° F.	27–30	160° F. (med.)
	6–8 lbs.	300–325° F.	32–35	170° F. (well)
Boneless rump roast	4–6 lbs.	300–325° F.	25–30	150–170° F.
Rib eye roast	4–6 lbs.	350° F.	18–20	140° F. (rare)
	4–6 lbs.	350° F.	20–22	160° F. (med.)
	4–6 lbs.	350° F.	22–24	170° F. (well)
Veal				
Loin	5 lbs.	300–325° F.	35–40	170° F.
Shoulder	6 lbs.	300–325° F.	25–30	170° F.
Lamb				
Leg	5–9 lbs.	300–325° F.	20–25	140° F. (rare)
	5–9 lbs.	300–325° F.	25–30	160° F. (med.)
	5–9 lbs.	300–325° F.	30–35	170° F. (well)
Crown roast	2¼–4 lbs.	300–325° F.	30–35	140° F. (rare)
	2¼–4 lbs.	300–325° F.	35–40	160° F. (med.)
	2¼–4 lbs.	300–325° F.	40–45	170–180° F. (well)
Shoulder				
Square cut	4–6 lbs.	300–325° F.	25–30	160° F. (med.)
	4–6 lbs.	300–325° F.	30–35	170–180° F. (well)
Boneless	3½–5 lbs.	300–325° F.	30–35	140° F. (rare)
	3½–5 lbs.	300–325° F.	35–40	160° F. (med.)
	3½–5 lbs.	300–325° F.	40–45	170–180° F. (well)
Pork, fresh				
Loin roast				
Center	3–5 lbs.	325–350° F.	30–35	170° F.
Half	5–7 lbs.	325–350° F.	35–40	170° F.
Crown roast	6–10 lbs.	325–350° F.	25–30	170° F.
Arm picnic shoulder				
Bone-in	5–8 lbs.	325–350° F.	30–35	170° F.
Boneless	3–5 lbs.	325–350° F.	35–40	170° F.
Country-style ribs, Spareribs, back-ribs	—	325–350° F.	1½–2 hrs.	—

◻ Roasting Meat

Kind of Meat	Ready-to-Cook Weight	Oven Temp.	Cooking Time (Min. per Lb.)	Internal Temp. of Meat When Done
Pork, smoked				
Ham (fully cooked)				
Whole (boneless)	8–12 lbs.	300–325° F.	15–18	130–140° F.
Whole (bone-in)	14–16 lbs.	300–325° F.	15–18	130–140° F.
Half (boneless)	4–6 lbs.	300–325° F.	18–25	130–140° F.
Half (bone-in)	7–8 lbs.	300–325° F.	18–25	130–140° F.
Portion (boneless)	3–4 lbs.	300–325° F.	27–33	130–140° F.
Ham (cook-before-eating)				
Whole (boneless)	8–12 lbs.	300–325° F.	17–21	160° F.
Whole (bone-in)	14–16 lbs.	300–325° F.	18–20	160° F.
Half (bone-in)	7–8 lbs.	300–325° F.	22–25	160° F.
Portion (bone-in)	3–5 lbs.	300–325° F.	35–40	160° F.

Sources: U.S. Dept. of Agriculture, National Live Stock and Meat Board.

Kind of Poultry	Ready-to-Cook Weight	Roasting Time (at 325° F.)
Chicken		
Broilers, fryers	1½–2½ lbs.	1–2 hrs.
Roasters, stuffed	2½–4½ lbs.	2–3½ hrs.*
Duck	4–6 lbs.	2–3 hrs.
Goose	6–8 lbs.	3–3½ hrs.
	8–12 lbs.	3½–4½ hrs.
Turkey		
Roasters, stuffed	6–8 lbs.	3–3½ hrs.*
	8–12 lbs.	3½–4½ hrs.*
	12–16 lbs.	4½–5½ hrs.*
	16–20 lbs.	5½–6½ hrs.*
	20–24 lbs.	6½–7 hrs.*
Halves, quarters and half breasts	3–8 lbs.	2–3 hrs.
	8–12 lbs.	3–4 hrs.
Boneless roasts	2–10 lbs.	2–4 hrs.

*Unstuffed poultry may take slightly less time.

Source: U.S. Dept. of Agriculture.

▭ Broiling Meat

Kind of Meat	Thickness or Weight	Cooking Time (Min.)
Beef		
Rib, rib eye, top loin steaks	1 in.	15 (rare)–20 (med.)
	1½ in.	25 (rare)–30 (med.)
	2 in.	35 (rare)–45 (med.)
Sirloin, porterhouse steaks	1 in.	20 (rare)–25 (med.)
	1½ in.	30 (rare)–35 (med.)
	2 in.	40 (rare)–45 (med.)
Filet mignon	4–8 oz.	10–15 (rare)–15–20 (med.)
Hamburger	1 in.	15 (rare)–25 (med.)
Lamb		
Rib, loin chops	1½ in.	18
	2 in.	22
Sirloin chops	¾–1 in.	12–14
Cubes for kabobs	1–1½ in.	12–18
	1½–2 in.	18–22
Ground lamb patties	1 in.	18
Pork, fresh		
Rib, loin, blade or sirloin chops	¾–1½ in.	30–45
Shoulder steaks	½–¾ in.	30–45
Country-style ribs, spareribs, backribs	—	1–1½ hrs.
Ground pork patties	½ in.	12–15
Cubes for kabobs	1–1¼ in.	26–32
Pork, smoked		
Ham slice	½ in.	10–12
Canadian bacon	½ in.	6–8

Source: National Live Stock and Meat Board.

Kind of Meat	Weight or Thickness	Cooking Time
Beef		
Pot roast	3–5 lbs.	2½–3½ hrs.
Short ribs	pieces	1½–2½ hrs.
Flank steak	1½–2 lbs.	1½–2½ hrs.
Stuffed steak	½–¾ in.	1½ hrs.
Round steak	¾–1 in.	1–1½ hrs.
Swiss steak	1½–2½ in.	2–3 hrs.
Veal		
Chops	½–¾ in.	45–60 min.
Cubes for stew	1 in.	1½–2 hrs.
Shoulder, rolled	3–5 lbs.	2–2½ hrs.
Steaks (cutlets)	½–¾ in.	45–60 min.
Lamb		
Shoulder chops	¾–1 in.	45–60 min.
Shanks	1 lb.	1½–2 hrs.
Pieces for stew	1½ in.	1½–2 hrs.
Pork, fresh		
Chops	¾–1½ in.	45–60 min.
Country-style ribs, spareribs, backribs	—	1½–2 hrs.
Tenderloin		
Whole	½–1 lb.	45–60 min.
Slices	½ in.	30 min.
Shoulder steaks	¾ in.	45–60 min.
Cubes for stew	1–1¼ in.	45–60 min.

Sources: U.S. Dept. of Agriculture, National Live Stock and Meat Board.

8 Ways to Cook Fish

1. Bake
- Place clean, dressed fish in a greased baking dish.
- To keep moist, brush with seasoned melted fat, a sauce or topping.
- Bake in moderate oven (350°F.) until fish flakes easily with a fork. (See charts, pp. 59–60.)

2. Broil
- Fish to be broiled should be at least 1″ thick.
- Arrange fish in a single layer on a well-greased broiler rack about 3–4″ from heat source.
- Baste fish well with melted fat or oil or a basting sauce before and during broiling.
- Turn thicker servings, such as steaks or whole fish, halfway through cooking time and baste again. (See charts, pp. 59–60.)

3. Charcoal Broil
- Select a barbecue with a closely spaced grill. Grease grill well.
- For smaller fillets, use a special fish grill or barbecue basket.
- Place fish 4″ from hot coals.
- Baste with marinade or barbecue sauce before and during cooking.
- Broil until fish flakes easily with a fork. (See chart, next page.)

4. Deep-fat Fry
- Use only very small fish or fillets.
- Dip fish into seasoned milk or beaten egg and then into crumbs, cornmeal or batter.
- Place a single layer of fish in a wire frying basket.
- In a deep kettle, heat enough fat to 350° F. to float the fish. Do not fill the kettle more than half full.
- Lower basket containing fish gently into kettle to prevent excess bubbling.
- Fry fish until they are lightly browned and flake easily when tested with a fork. (See chart, next page.)
- Drain on absorbent paper.
- Before frying additional fish, be sure fat returns to 350° F.

5. Ovenfry
- Dip fish servings in seasoned milk or beaten egg and then into crumbs, cornmeal or flour.
- Bake in a pre-heated oven until fish flake easily when tested with a fork. (See chart, next page.)

6. Panfry
- Dip clean, dressed small fish into milk or beaten egg and then into cracker crumbs, cornmeal or flour.
- Heat about ⅛″ of fat in the bottom of a heavy fry pan.
- Place breaded fish in a single layer in hot fat.
- Fry fish until lightly browned on each side and fish flake easily when tested with a fork. (See chart, next page.)

7. Poach
- Place a single layer of fish in a wide, shallow pan (like a fry pan).
- Barely cover fish with a liquid such as lightly salted water or milk.
- Bring liquid to a boil, reduce heat and simmer until fish flake easily. (See chart, next page.)

8. Steam
- Use a steam cooker or a deep pot with a tight cover. The pot should be deep enough to hold a wire basket or rack and keep the fish above the liquid.
- Pour about 2″ of seasoned or plain water into the pot.
- Bring water to a rapid boil.
- Place fish on the rack or in the basket.
- Cover pot tightly and steam fish until it flakes easily. (See chart, next page.)

Sources: National Marine Fisheries Service, National Fisheries Inst., Inc.

Cooking Fish

Method	Market Form	Cooking Temp.	Approx. Cooking Time (Min.)
Baking	Dressed	350° F.	45–60
	Pan-dressed	350° F.	25–30
	Fillets or steaks	350° F.	20–25
	Frozen sticks	400° F.	15–20
Broiling	Pan-dressed	—	10–16 (turning once)
	Fillets or steaks	—	10–15
	Frozen fish sticks	—	10–15
Charcoal broiling	Pan-dressed	Moderate	10–16 (turning once)
	Fillets or steaks	Moderate	10–16 (turning once)
	Frozen fish sticks	Moderate	8–10 (turning once)
Deep-fat frying	Pan-dressed	350° F.	3–5
	Fillets or steaks	350° F.	3–5
Oven-frying	Pan-dressed	500° F.	15–20
	Fillets or steaks	500° F.	10–15
Pan-frying	Pan-dressed	Moderate	8–10 (turning once)
	Fillets or steaks	Moderate	8–10 (turning once)
	Frozen fish sticks	Moderate	8–10 (turning once)
Poaching	Fillets or steaks	Simmer	5–10
Steaming	Fillets or steaks	Boil	5–10

Source: National Marine Fisheries Service.

🗂 Cooking Shellfish

Fish	Broiling Time (Min.)	Baking Temp./ Time (Min.)
Clams		
Live	4–5	450° F./10–15
Shucked	4–5	350° F./8–10
Crabs	–	350° F./8–10
Lobsters	12–15	400° F./20–25
Oysters		
Live	4–5	450° F./10–15
Shucked	4–5	350° F./8–10
Scallops	6–8	350° F./20–25
Shrimp	8–10	350° F./20–25

Source: National Marine Fisheries Service.

Cooking Fresh Vegetables 🗂

Vegetable	Steam (Min.)	Boil (Min.)
Artichokes		
French or globe	30–45	30–45
Jerusalem, slices	—	15–30
Asparagus		
Spears	12–16	10–15
Tips	7–10	5–10
Beans		
Lima	25–35	12–20
Green (whole)	20–35	15–30
(French-cut)	15–25	10–20
Beets (whole)	40–60	30–45
Broccoli (split stalks)	15–20	10–15
Brussels sprouts (whole)	15–20	10–20
Cabbage		
Green (quartered)	15	10–15
(shredded)	8–12	3–10
Red (shredded)	10–15	8–12
Carrots		
Whole	20–30	15–20
Sliced, diced	15–25	10–20
Cauliflower		
Whole	25–30	15–25
Flowerets	10–20	8–15
Celery (sliced)	25–30	15–18
Collards	—	10–20
Corn		
On cob	10–15	6–12
Kernels	10–12	6–8

🗔 Cooking Fresh Vegetables

Vegetable	Steam (Min.)	Boil (Min.)
Eggplant (sliced)	15–20	10–20
Kale	15	10–15
Okra (sliced)	20	10–15
Onions		
Small (whole)	25–35	15–30
Large (whole)	35–40	20–40
Parsnips		
Whole	30–45	20–40
Quartered	30–40	8–15
Peas	10–20	12–16
Potatoes		
Whole	30–45	25–40
Quartered	20–30	20–25
Rutabaga (diced)	35–40	20–30
Spinach	5–12	3–10
Squash		
Acorn (quartered)	25–40	18–20
Butternut (cubed)	20–35	16–18
Summer (sliced)	15–20	8–15
Sweet potatoes		
Whole	30–35	35–55
Quartered	25–30	15–25
Turnips		
Whole	—	20–30
Sliced	20–25	15–20

Source: U.S. Dept. of Agriculture.

Spice and Herb Chart 🔲

Spice/Herb	Where to Use
Allspice	Baked goods and desserts, especially fruit; sweet potatoes, squash, turnips. Use whole in pickling and marinades. *Tip:* add a dash of ground allspice to cranberry cocktail.
Anise seed	Baked goods, especially cookies and fruit pies; great in orange sauce for chicken, duck.
Basil leaves	Cooked vegetables, poultry, seafood, salads; especially good with any tomato-based dish.
Bay leaves	Soups, stews, casseroles, sauces; use 1 large or 2 small leaves per 6 portions of meat, fowl, fish or seafood. *Tip:* add a few bay leaves to the skewer, alternating them with beef or lamb cubes, when preparing kabobs.
Caraway seed	Cheese dips and spreads, sauerbraten, sauerkraut, pork dishes; good with cabbage, carrots and cheese. *Tip:* add to melted butter for noodles and pasta.
Cardamon seed	Combine with other sweet spices (cloves, nutmeg, cinnamon) for coffee cakes, cookies, buns, pumpkin and apple pies. *Tips:* sprinkle ground cardamon on honeydew melon. Add whole seed to demi-tasse coffee.
Celery seed	Meat loaf, stews, croquettes, salads and dressings. *Tips:* add seeds liberally to cole slaw. Try a dash of ground celery seed in scrambled eggs.
Chervil leaves	Salads, stuffings, sauces, omelets, seafood and cheese dips. *Tip:* mix into canned or frozen peas as they are being heated.

Spice and Herb Chart

Spice/Herb	Where to Use
Chili powder	Chili con-carne, Mexican dishes, cocktail sauces, egg dishes, stews, meatballs, meat loaves.
Chives	Eggs, sour cream-dressed baked potatoes, cottage cheese, cooked vegetables, cocktail dips, creamy sauces, salad dressings. *Tip:* sprinkle over vichyssoise and other cream soups as they are served.
Cinnamon	Baked goods, puddings, sweet sauces, frozen desserts. *Tips:* add some ground cinnamon to mashed sweet potatoes. Use a stick in beef stew or in hot apple cider, Irish coffee or espresso.
Cloves	Baked goods, with fruits or sweet yellow vegetables, ham and pork roasts. *Tips:* poke whole cloves into pork butt. Add to tomato sauce. Add a dash of ground cloves to canned beets.
Coriander seed	Cookies, cakes, biscuits, gingerbread batter, poultry stuffings, mixed green salads.
Cumin seed	Deviled eggs, soups, sauerkraut, pork, cheese dishes.
Dill seed	Sour cream- and mayonnaise-based sauces, dressings and salads. Good with fish, cauliflower, green beans, cabbage, new potatoes. *Tip:* crush seeds and add to homemade potato salad.
Dill weed	Green salads, vegetables, fish and seafood sauces, creamed chicken, marinades for beef or seafood, cottage cheese, egg salad.
Fennel seed	Chicken and seafood sauces, pork dishes, breads, rolls, coffee cakes. Good with celery, sweet vegetables, and apples in any form.

Spice/Herb	Where to Use
Garlic (dehydrated)	Use discreetly in meat, fowl and seafood; salad dressings; soups; sauces; appetizers. Use bravely in Mediterranean dishes—scampi, spaghetti sauces, Italian salads and dressings, bouillabaisse.
Ginger	Gingerbread, spice cakes and cookies. Enhances beef and chicken dishes, sauces and marinades. Use in seasoned flour for frying chicken and liver.
Mace	Called the "pound cake spice," it's also good in cherry pie, light fruit cakes, sweet vegetables, fish sauces, seafood chowders, creamed spinach or chicken.
Marjoram leaves	Roast meats of all kinds, poultry, fish, green vegetables, salads, herbed breads.
Mint	Desserts, teas and drinks; over tossed green salads; with carrots and pickled beets and fruit. Much used with lamb and in Greek cooking.
Mustard seed	*Ground:* cheese dishes, Welsh rarebit, ham salad, creamed vegetables, meat sauces. *Whole seed:* pickling, salad dressings, marinades.
Nutmeg	Cakes, cookies, pies, puddings, eggnog, custards, any lemon dessert. Very good with corn, creamed spinach, chicken, seafood.
Onion (dehydrated)	In meats, poultry, seafood, salads especially. Also vegetables of all kinds, soups, sauces, omelets and egg dishes.
Oregano leaves	Pizza, spaghetti sauce, other Italian dishes. Use with meat, cheese, fish, eggs and in marinades. Ideal with fresh and cooked tomatoes, zucchini, green beans.

☐ Spice and Herb Chart

Spice/Herb	Where to Use
Paprika	As a garnish and flavor for all kinds of creamed and light-colored foods, like Welsh rarebit, deviled eggs, mayonnaise dressings, white potatoes, cauliflower, salads, dips, canapes, chowders. *Tip:* coat fish steaks lightly with mayonnaise and liberally sprinkle with paprika before broiling.
Parsley	In butter sauces for meats, poultry, fish, vegetables; scrambled eggs; stuffings; soups and chowders; salads and dressings.
Pepper, black	"The world's favorite spice" is good in all kinds of meat, vegetable dishes; even in spice cakes, cookies (pfeffernusse), mincemeat, pumpkin pies.
Pepper, white	Uses comparable to black pepper, but preferred in light-colored foods and sauces, like creamed preparations, chowders, egg and cheese dishes.
Pepper, red	*Ground:* dips, sauces, soups, meats. *Crushed:* Italian-style loaf sandwiches, on pizza and spaghetti, in Mexican dishes.
Rosemary leaves	Roast or broiled lamb, chicken, beef, pork; in sauces for fish, salads, dressings; with eggplant, green beans, summer squash, mushrooms.
Saffron	With rice, chicken and seafood in soups, chowders, casseroles; also in European recipes for cakes and breads. *Tip:* place a pinch in boiling water before adding rice to develop golden color and appetizing flavor.
Sage leaves	In stuffings, meat loaves, pork sausage and pork dishes generally; also in fish chowders. melted cheese dishes, pizza sauce.

Spice and Herb Chart

Spice/Herb	Where to Use
Savory leaves	With green beans, meat, chicken, dressings, scrambled eggs and omelets; also in soups, salads and sauces.
Sesame seeds	Use in place of finely chopped nutmeats in and on cakes, cookies, cream pies, breads. Good in stuffings, meat loaves, tossed salads, and in butters for vegetables. *Tip:* mix liberally into stuffing for roast turkey.
Tarragon leaves	In salad dressings and sauces for meat, poultry or seafood; also in tartar sauce, egg and tomato dishes. *Tip:* add ground or crumbled leaves to the dressing for chicken salad.
Thyme leaves	With clam chowders, seafood, stuffings, in creamed chicken or chipped beef, and over white onions, eggplant, tomatoes, celery. *Tip:* sprinkle a pinch of crumbled leaves over sliced tomatoes and add oil and vinegar.
Tumeric	Adds saffron-like natural coloring in main dishes that contain rice, chicken, seafood or eggs.

Source: American Spice Trade Assn.

▢ Wine Companion Chart

Food	Wine	Serving Temp.
Appetizers		
Smoked salmon, almonds, olives, hors d'oeuvres, canapes; as an apertif	Champagne, dry sherry, white (dry) port, dry Madeira, white or red vermouth, Mantilla	Well chilled
Oysters	Chablis, Muscadet, Pinot Blanc	Well chilled
Clams	Dry sherry, Pinot Blanc	Well chilled
Soups		
Consomme or turtle soup	Madeira, medium sherry	Room temperature
Heavy vegetable soups, pot-au-feu, oxtail soup	Beaujolais, Pinot Noir	Room temperature
Eggs, pasta		
Omelettes, quiche, egg dishes	Champagne, dry Rhine wines, Moselles	Cold
Pasta dishes with tomato sauce	Chianti, Barbera, Bardolino Valpolicella	Cool or room temperature
Main dishes		
Barbecue: chicken	Vin Rose; light, dry white wines like Soave, Frascati, California Chablis	Well chilled
Barbecue: beef	Beaujolais, Zinfandel	Cool
Fish, poached or grilled; crab; lobster	White Bordeaux, Fume Blanc, Sauvignon Blanc, light white Burgundy, Pouilly-Fuisse, Pinot Chardonnay, dry Graves, Moselle, Soave, Frascati, Orvieto, Verdicchio	Well chilled
Chicken; rich fish or shellfish dishes; cold fowl or cold meats	Full white, Burgundies, Graves, Rhine wine, Gewurztraminer, California Pinot Chardonnay	Well chilled
Roast turkey	Red Bordeaux, St. Emillion or Pomerol, California Cabernet	Room temperature
Roast ham or pork	Vin Rose or a full German wine like Riesling or Rhine wine; Bordeaux	Well chilled

Food	Wine	Serving Temp.
Main dishes (continued)		
Veal	Light red Bordeaux, Beaujolais, California Cabernet or French Loire wines, California Chablis, Soave, Verdicchio	Cool or room temperature
Lamb	Red Bordeaux, California Cabernet	Room temperature
Beef, pheasant	St. Emilion or Pomerol; light red Burgundy, California Cabernet or Pinot Noir; Italian reds like Barbaresco, Barolo, Chianti Classico Riserva; Bordeaux	Room temperature
Stews, pot roast	Beaujolais, California Zinfandel or Gamay	Cool or room temperature
Game (venison, wild duck); steak	Hearty red Burgundy, Hermitage, Chateauneuf-du-Pape, Pinot Noire, Barolo, Barbaresco	Room temperature
Cheese		
Light cheese	Sauterne	Well chilled
Medium cheese	Cabernet Sauvignon, red Bordeaux	Room temperature
Sharp cheese	Chianti Classico Riserva, Barbaresco, Barolo, Garrinara, Amarone, Pinot Noir	Cool or room temperature
Desserts		
Desserts, pastries, fruit	Sweet Sauternes, Anjou, Spatlese Rhine wines, Champagne, Asti Spumanti	Well chilled
Nuts	Ruby port, sweet Madeira, cream sherry	Room temperature

Source: Italian Wine Center; Haskell's, Minneapolis.

Basic Drink-Making Guide

Key:
⅔ jigger = 1 oz.
1 jigger = 1½ oz.   ⅓ jigger = ½ oz.

Alexander

1 part fresh cream
1 part Creme de Cacao
1 part brandy
Shake thoroughly with cracked ice. Strain into cocktail glass.

Bloody Mary

2 jiggers tomato juice
⅓ jigger fresh lemon juice
Dash of Worchestershire sauce
1 jigger vodka
Salt and pepper to taste
Shake with cracked ice. Strain in 6 oz. glass.

Daiquiri

Juice of ½ lime or ¼ lemon
1 tsp. sugar
1 jigger light rum
Shake with cracked ice until shaker frosts.
Strain into cocktail glass.

Gimlet

4 parts gin or vodka
1 part Rose's sweetened lime juice
Shake with cracked ice and strain into a cocktail glass.
Garnish with slice of fresh lime.

Gin and Tonic

Juice and rind of ¼ lime
1 jigger gin
Quinine (tonic) water
Squeeze lime over ice cubes in tall glass and add rind. Pour in gin; fill with tonic water and stir.

Grasshopper

½ jigger fresh cream
⅔ jigger white Creme de Cacao
⅔ jigger green Creme de Menthe
Shake with cracked ice or mix in electric blender. Strain into cocktail glass.

Manhattan

1 jigger Bourbon or rye
⅓ jigger sweet vermouth
Dash of bitters (optional)
Stir with cracked ice and strain into glass. Add a cherry.

Margarita

1 jigger tequila
⅓ jigger Triple Sec
⅔ jigger fresh lime or lemon juice
Shake ingredients with cracked ice. Moisten rim of cocktail glass with fruit rind and spin rim in salt. Strain drink into salt-dipped glass.

Martini

4 parts gin or vodka
1 part dry vermouth
Stir with cracked ice and strain into chilled cocktail glass. Or serve on ice. Garnish with green olive or twist of lemon peel.

Old Fashioned

½ tsp. sugar
1 tsp. water
Dash of bitters
1 jigger whiskey
Mix sugar, water and bitters in Old Fashioned glass. Add ice, pour whiskey over and stir.

Pina Colada

1 jigger rum
⅔ jigger cream of coconut
1⅓ jigger unsweetened pineapple juice
Shake with ½ cup crushed ice. Pour into tall glass filled with ice cubes. Add a cherry.

Screwdriver

1 jigger vodka
Orange juice
Put ice cubes into 6 oz. glass. Add vodka; fill with orange juice and stir.

Sour

1 jigger Bourbon or rye
½ jigger fresh lemon juice
1 tsp. sugar
Shake with cracked ice and strain into glass. Add an orange slice and a cherry.

Stinger

1 jigger brandy
⅔ jigger white Creme de Menthe
Shake with cracked ice. Strain into glass.

Tom Collins

½ jigger fresh lemon juice
1 jigger gin
1 tsp. sugar
Sparkling water
In a tall glass, dissolve the sugar in the lemon juice; add ice cubes and gin. Fill with sparkling water. Stir.

Source: Distilled Spirits Council of the United States, Inc.

Chapter 3

EATING BETTER

🍎 What's a Healthy Diet?

This "New American Diet" gives you suggested daily servings of the basic four food groups. Use it to plan your daily menu.

Anytime: The "anytime" foods should be the backbone of your diet. They are low in fat (less than 30% of a food's calories) and low in sugar and salt. Grain foods are mostly unrefined whole grains and therefore are high in fiber and trace minerals.

In Moderation. The "in moderation" foods contain moderate amounts of either saturated or unsaturated fats. Some items contain large amounts of fat, but mostly monounsaturated or polyunsaturated types.

Now & Then. The "now & then" foods are usually high in saturated fat or very high in sugar, salt or cholesterol.

Food Group	Anytime	In Moderation	Now & Then
Beans, Grains & Nuts *4 or more servings per day*	bread & rolls (whole grain) bulghur dried beans & peas (legumes) lentils oatmeal pasta, whole wheat rice, brown rye bread sprouts whole grain hot & cold cereals whole wheat matzoh	cornbread flour tortilla granola cereals hominy grits macaroni and cheese matzoh nuts, seeds pasta, except whole wheat peanut butter pizza refined, unsweetened cereals refried beans soybeans, tofu waffles or pancakes with syrup white bread and rolls white rice	croissant doughnut (yeast-leavened) presweetened breakfast cereals sticky buns stuffing (made with butter)
Fruits & Vegetables *4 or more servings per day*	all fruits and vegetables except those listed at right applesauce (unsweetened) unsweetened fruit juices unsalted vegetable juices potatoes, white or sweet	avocado cole slaw cranberry sauce (canned) dried fruit french fries fried eggplant (vegetable oil) fruits canned in syrup gazpacho, guacamole glazed carrots potatoes au gratin salted vegetable juices sweeted fruit juices vegetables canned with salt	coconut pickles

Food Group	Anytime	In Moderation	Now & Then
Milk Products *Children: 3–4 servings per day* *Adults: 2 servings per day*	buttermilk made from skim milk low-fat cottage cheese low-fat milk, 1% milkfat low-fat yogurt non-fat dry milk skim milk cheeses skim milk skim milk & banana shake	cocoa made with skim milk cottage cheese, regular, 4% milkfat frozen lowfat yogurt ice milk low-fat milk, 2% milkfat low-fat yogurt, sweetened mozzarella cheese, part-skim type only	·cheesecake cheese fondue cheese souffle eggnog hard cheeses, bleu, brick, camembert, cheddar, muenster, swiss ice cream processed cheeses whole milk whole milk yogurt
Poultry, Fish, Meat & Eggs *2 servings per day*	FISH cod flounder gefilte fish haddock halibut perch pollock rockfish shellfish, except shrimp sole tuna, water-packed EGG PRODUCTS egg whites only POULTRY chicken or turkey broiled, baked or roasted (no skin)	FISH (drained well, if canned) fried fish herring mackerel, canned salmon, pink, canned sardines shrimp tuna, oil-packed POULTRY chicken liver, baked or broiled. (just one!) fried chicken, homemade in vegetable oil chicken or turkey, boiled, baked, or roasted (with skin) RED MEATS (trimmed of all outside fat) flank steak leg or loin of lamb pork shoulder or loin lean round steak or ground round rump roast sirloin steak, lean veal	POULTRY fried chicken, commercially prepared EGG cheese omelet egg yolk or whole egg (about 3 per week) RED MEATS bacon beef liver, fried bologna corned beef ground beef ham, trimmed well hot dogs liverwurst pig's feet salami sausage spareribs untrimmed red meats

Source: Center for Science in the Public Interest. A full-color poster of the "New American Eating Guide" is available for $2.50 from the CSPI, 1755 S St. NW, Washington, DC 20009.

◖ What You Need to Know About the Basic Nutrients

Everybody needs daily or periodic doses of the basic nutrients—protein, carbohydrates, fats, vitamins and minerals. The charts on the following pages identify these nutrients, describe what they do for your body, and list some good food sources. The charts also identify the possible consequences of getting too little or too much of a particular nutrient. If you eat a balanced diet each day, drawing on foods from each of the four basic groups (see previous page), you'll get all the nutrients you need. Large (or mega-) doses of some nutrients, like fat-soluble vitamins, are not only *not* helpful—they may do harm.

Proteins, Carbohydrates and Fats Guide

Nutrient	What It Does	Extreme Effects	Good Food Sources
Protein	• Provides the amino acids necessary for building and maintaining body cells. • Produces hemoglobin in the blood. • Helps make the antibodies used to fight infection. • Is made up of 22 different amino acids, most of which the body can make, but 9 of which need to be eaten in order for the body to get adequate amounts. These nine are called the "essential amino acids."	• **Too little:** Poorly formed or deteriorated muscles, organs and brain tissue; poor teeth, hair and bones; anemia, malnutrition and inability of the blood to clot. • **Too much:** Kidney disease and loss of calcium from the body.	Fish, poultry, meat. Also, non-meat sources such as eggs, milk, cheese or any one of the following combinations: corn and beans; peanut butter and wheat bread; cereal and milk; dried beans or peas with rice, corn or any grain or cereal; nuts or peanuts with grains or rice; seeds with legumes; macaroni and cheese; rice with milk. (See also p. 83.)
Carbo-hydrates	• Provide a major source of energy. • Ensure normal fat metabolism. • Consist of 2 types: starches (complex carbohydrates) and simple sugars. • Many sources provide essential nutrients and dietary fiber (see below).	• **Too little:** Loss of organ or muscle tissue (built of protein) to supply energy, thus causing physical deterioration. • **Too much:** Obesity.	Starches and simple sugars are both found in their most nutritious form in unrefined cereals, whole-grain breads, rice, dried beans, milk, fruits and vegetables. Many refined foods are also sources of starches and simple sugars, but many nutrients and much of the fiber has been processed out of them—as in cookies, candies, cakes, pies, potato chips and other similar snack foods.

Proteins, Carbohydrates and Fats Guide ♥

Nutrient	What It Does	Extreme Effects	Good Food Sources
Fats	• Serve as the body's most concentrated source of energy and fatty acids. • Provide a protective cushion around vital body organs. • Insulate the body and therefore help control body temperature. • Act as an internal lubricant. • Aid in utilizing fat-soluble vitamins (A, D, E and K).	• **Too little:** Deficiencies in vitamins A, D, E and K. • **Too much:** Obesity, cardiovascular disease, diabetes.	Cooking oils and fats, butter, margarine, salad dressings; bacon, sausage and other fatty meats; cream and most cheeses.
Fiber (not considered an essential nutrient)	• Adds bulk to the diet. • Acts as a laxative.	• **Too little:** Constipation; in some cases, hemorrhoids and even diverticular disease. • **Too much:** Vitamin and mineral deficiency; flatulence.	Whole-grain breads, bran and grain cereals, apples, raw carrots, corn, raw celery, cooked lentils and kidney beans, peas, potatoes, parsnips, leafy vegetables.

Sources: Food and Drug Administration, U.S. Dept. of Agriculture.

🍎 Vitamin Guide

Fat-Soluble Vitamins (A, D, E and K): are absorbed into the body with the aid of fats consumed in the diet. These vitamins are stored in the body, so daily doses are not necessary.

Vitamin	What It Does	Extreme Effects	Good Food Sources
Vitamin A	• Aids new cell growth and maintenance of healthy tissues, especially the linings of the mouth, nose, throat, and digestive and urinary tracts. • Is essential for vision in dim light.	• **Too little:** Night blindness, high sensitivity to light and other eye problems; rough, dry skin. • **Too much:** Swelling of feet and ankles, fatigue, weight loss, superficial hemorrhages in the retinae, skin lesions, thinning of the hair.	Liver, dark green leafy vegetables (chard, cress, broccoli, collard), yellow vegetables (carrots, winter squash, pumpkin), apricots, cantaloupe. (See also p. 83.)
Vitamin D	• Aids in the absorption of calcium and phosphorus in bone and teeth formation.	• **Too little:** Rickets, soft bones, bowed legs, poor teeth, bone deformities and multiple fractures. • **Too much:** Loss of appetite, thirst, lethargy, excessive urination, nausea and vomiting, diarrhea and constipation, weight loss, elevated calcium and phosphorus levels, calcium deposits, kidney stones.	Canned and fresh fish (esp. salt water varieties), egg yolk, fortified milk.
Vitamin E	• Prevents oxygen from destroying other substances, such as Vitamin A. • Aids in the formation of red blood cells, muscles and other tissues.	• **Too little:** No clinical effects associated with low intake. • **Too much:** Headache, nausea, giddiness, fatigue, blurred vision, deficiency of Vitamin K.	Vegetable oils, dry beans, eggs, whole grains, liver, fruits, green leafy vegetables.
Vitamin K	• Aids in blood coagulation.	• **Too little:** Hemorrhages and liver injury. • **Too much:** Anemia.	Spinach, lettuce, kale, cabbage, cauliflower, liver, egg yolks.

Water-Soluble Vitamins (the B vitamins and C): are not stored in the body and must be consumed in adequate amounts daily.

Vitamin	What It Does	Extreme Effects	Good Food Sources
Vitamin B_1 (Thiamin)	• Aids in normal digestion, growth, fertility, lactation and normal functioning of nerve tissues. • Helps convert sugar and starches to energy.	• **Too little:** Poor appetite, constipation, irritability, insomnia, fatigue, beriberi, swelling of the body (edema), heart problems. • **Too much:** None known.	Whole grains and enriched cereals and breads, dry beans and green peas, fish, pork, lean meats, poultry, liver. (See also p. 83.)
Vitamin B_2 (Riboflavin)	• Helps the body obtain energy from carbohydrates and proteins.	• **Too little:** Lip sores and cracks in the corners of the mouth; red, scaly areas around the nose; high sensitivity to light; dimness of vision. • **Too much:** None known.	Milk, cheese, eggs, liver, kidney, mushrooms, green leafy vegetables, lean meats, enriched breads and cereals, dry beans. (See also p. 83.)
Vitamin B_3 (Niacin)	• Works with other vitamins to convert carbohydrates into energy. • Helps in the maintenance of all tissue cells.	• **Too little:** Pellegra (swollen, beef-red tongue), loss of appetite, diarrhea, depression, laziness, dermatitis. • **Too much:** High blood sugar, abnormal liver function, gastrointestinal complaints.	Liver, lean meats, peas, dry beans, enriched and whole-grain cereal products. (See also p. 83.)
Vitamin B_6	• Aids in the metabolism and synthesis of proteins, fats and carbohydrates. • Assists proper growth and maintenance of body functions.	• **Too little:** Mouth soreness, dizziness, nausea, weight loss. • **Too much:** Dependency on high doses.	Liver, whole-grain cereals, wheat germ, potatoes, red meats, green leafy vegetables, yellow corn.
Vitamin B_{12}	• Aids in the development of red blood cells and the functioning of all cells, particularly in the bone marrow, nervous system and intestines.	• **Too little:** Pernicious anemia and, if deficiency is prolonged, a degeneration of the spinal cord. • **Too much:** None known.	Liver, kidney, lean meats, fish, milk, eggs, shellfish.
Folic Acid (Folacin)	• Helps the body manufacture red blood cells. • Helps convert food to energy.	• **Too little:** Anemia, diarrhea, smooth tongue. • **Too much:** None known.	Green leafy vegetables, liver, kidney, navy beans, nuts, oranges, wheat germ.

⊘ Vitamin Guide

Water-Soluble Vitamins (the B vitamins and C): are not stored in the body and must be consumed in adequate amounts daily.

Vitamin	What It Does	Extreme Effects	Good Food Sources
Pantothenic Acid	• Supports a variety of body functions, including proper growth and maintenance. • Aids in the metabolism of carbohydrates and fats.	• **Too little:** Headache, fatigue, poor muscle coordination, nausea, cramps. • **Too much:** Need for extra thiamin.	Liver, eggs, potatoes, peas, whole grains, peanuts, brewer's yeast.
Biotin	• Helps synthesize fatty acids. • Aids in the metabolism of carbohydrates, fats and protein.	• **Too little:** Mild skin disorders, anemia, depression, loss of appetite, nausea, sleeplessness, muscle pain. • **Too much:** None known.	Egg yolks, milk, meats, liver, kidney, brown rice, lentils, sardines, brewer's yeast.
Vitamin C (Ascorbic Acid)	• Aids in tissue repair, including the healing of wounds. • Assists in the formation of intercellular substances, connective tissue, cartilage, bones, teeth and blood vessels. • Aids in calcium absorption.	• **Too little:** Scurvy (weakness, loss of weight, bleeding gums, irritability); tendency to bruise easily; painful, swollen joints. • **Too much:** Insomnia, high blood pressure, nausea, headache, kidney and bladder stones, dependency on high doses.	Oranges, grapefruit, strawberries, cantaloupe, tomatoes, peppers, potatoes, cabbage, broccoli, brussels sprouts, asparagus, green peas, kale. (See also p. 83.)

Sources: Food and Drug Administration; U.S. Dept. of Agriculture; Dairy, Food and Nutrition Council of Minnesota.

Mineral Guide 🍎

Macrominerals (such as calcium, magnesium, phosphorus, potassium, sodium and sulfur): are found in relatively large amounts in the body. You need fairly high amounts of them in your diet (more than 100 milligrams per day).

Mineral	What It Does	Extreme Effects	Good Food Sources
Calcium	• Works with phosphorus to make hard bones and teeth. • Controls blood clotting and normal response of muscles and nerves.	• **Too little:** Rickets, a decreased rate of growth, and osteoporosis (deteriorated bones). • **Too much:** Calcium deposits in the body, drowsiness.	Milk, cheese, yogurt, ice cream, dark green leafy vegetables (broccoli, spinach, kale, mustard greens, turnip greens), molasses, almonds, dried beans. (See also p. 83).
Magnesium	• Makes proteins in the body, releases muscle energy, builds bones and conducts nerve impulses. • Helps the body adjust to cold temperatures.	• **Too little:** Weakness, insomnia, muscle cramps, twitching and tremors, shakiness, irregular heartbeat. • **Too much:** An imbalance with calcium.	Green leafy vegetables, almonds and cashews, soybeans, seeds, whole grains.
Phosphorus	• Helps develop and maintain strong bones and teeth. • Maintains alkalinity of the blood.	• **Too little:** Rickets, weakness. • **Too much:** An imbalance with calcium, calcium deficiency.	Wheat germ, cheese, mustard, milk, egg yolks, brewer's yeast, dried beans and peas, nuts, whole grains (rye, barley), turkey, codfish, rice, cottage cheese.
Potassium	• Maintains electrolyte and fluid balance in the cells. • Transmits nerve impulses and helps in muscle contractions and the release of energy from foods.	• **Too little:** Laziness, abnormal heart rhythms, weakness, kidney and lung failure. • **Too much:** Abnormal heart rhythms.	Bananas, raisins, seeds (sesame, sunflower, etc.), orange juice, dried fruits, dried beans and peas, potatoes, meats.
Sodium	• Maintains blood volume and the proper amount of pressure in the cells for transmitting nerve impulses.	• **Too little:** An electrolyte imbalance. • **Too much:** High blood pressure and heart disease, kidney disease, stroke, edema (water retention and swelling).	Table salt, nearly all processed foods, olives (green and ripe), sauerkraut, pickles (dill and sweet), hominy, celery, beet greens, chard, soy sauce.
Sulfur	• Promotes healthy skin, hair and nails.	• **Too little:** None known. • **Too much:** None known.	Beets, wheat germ, dried beans and peas, peanuts, clams.

◌ Mineral Guide

Trace minerals (such as copper, iodine, iron, manganese and zinc): are found in extremely small amounts in the body. You need only tiny amounts of them in your daily diet.

Mineral	What It Does	Extreme Effects	Good Food Sources
Copper	• Helps use and store iron to form hemoglobin for red blood cells.	• **Too little:** Retarded growth, anemia, respiratory problems. • **Too much:** Diarrhea, vomiting.	Plentiful in most unprocessed foods, especially dried beans, nuts, shellfish, organ meats.
Iodine	• Promotes normal functioning of the thyroid gland.	• **Too little:** Goiter. • **Too much:** None known.	Iodized salt, seafood.
Iron	• Makes hemoglobin. • Helps cells get energy from food.	• **Too little:** Anemia. • **Too much:** Toxic levels in the body.	Liver, egg yolks, shellfish, lean meats, green leafy vegetables, peas, dried beans, dried fruits, molasses, whole-grain cereals. (See also p. 83.)
Manganese	• Forms and maintains normal bones and tendons.	• **Too little:** None known. • **Too much:** Blurred speech, tremors.	Plentiful in many foods, especially bran, tea, coffee, nuts, peas, beans.
Zinc	• Helps move carbon dioxide from the tissues to the lungs, where it's exhaled.	• **Too little:** Loss of sense of taste, slow healing of wounds. • **Too much:** Nausea, vomiting, abdominal pain, anemia.	Lean meat, fish, egg yolks, milk.

Sources: Food and Drug Administration, U.S. Dept. of Agriculture.

What Food Labels Tell You

• **Ingredients.** Ingredients must be listed in descending order of prominence by weight. The first ingredients listed are the main ingredients in that product.

• **Color and flavors.** Added colors and flavors do not have to be listed by name, but the use of artificial colors or flavors must be indicated. Artificial color need not be noted for butter, cheese and ice cream, however.

• **Serving content.** For each serving: the serving size; the number of calories per serving; the amount of protein, carbohydrates and fat in a serving; the percentage of the U.S. Recommended Daily Allowance (U.S. RDA) for protein and 7 important vitamins and minerals. (See the following page for a discussion of the U.S. RDAs.)

• **Optional information.** Some labels also contain the following: the percentage of the USRDA for any of 12 additional vitamins and minerals; the amount of saturated and unsaturated fat and cholesterol in a serving; the amount of sodium furnished by a serving; and a breakdown of the kinds of carbohydrates in a serving.

What Food Labels Don't Tell You

• **What standardized foods contain.** Over 350 foods, including common ones like enriched white bread and catsup, are classified as "standardized" (for which the FDA has established guidelines). Manufacturers are not required to list ingredients for these products.

• **How much sugar is in some products.** Sugars and sweeteners come in a variety of forms (white sugar, brown sugar, corn syrup, dextrose, sucrose, maltose, corn sweeteners), and if they're all listed separately, it's nearly impossible to know the true amount of sugar contained in a labeled product.

• **How "natural" a product is.** The FDA's policy on using the word "natural" on a food label is loose. The product may, in fact, be highly processed and full of additives.

• **Specific ingredients that may be harmful.** Since colorings or spices that don't have to be listed by name can cause nausea, dizziness or hives in certain people, people with food or additive allergies don't know which products they need to avoid.

Sources: Food and Drug Administration; *Nutrition Action* (published by the Center for Science in the Public Interest; membership is available to the public for $20.00 per year).

🍎 U.S. Recommended Daily Allowances (U.S. RDAs)

The U.S. RDAs (Table 1) were developed by the Food and Drug Administration for nutrition labeling purposes. They represent 100% of what might be recommended (not required) for a child or adult in most circumstances. However, as you can see from Table 2, not all people need 100% of every nutrient every day; in fact, some need far less, and in special circumstances, like pregnancy, some need more.

Table 1—U.S. RDAs

Protein	65 gm
Vitamin A	5,000 IU
Vitamin C	60 mg
Vitamin B$_1$ (Thiamin)	1.5 mg
Vitamin B$_2$ (Riboflavin)	1.7 mg
Vitamin B$_3$ (Niacin)	20 mg
Calcium	1.0 gm
Iron	18 mg

(gm = gram; IU = International Unit; mg = milligram.)

Table 2—Percentage of the U.S. RDAs (of protein and 7 important vitamins and minerals) for Different Ages and Sexes

Age	Protein	Vitamin A	Vitamin C	Vitamin B$_1$ (Thiamin)	Vitamin B$_2$ (Riboflavin)	Vitamin B$_3$ (Niacin)	Calcium	Iron
Child:								
1–3	35	40	75	50	50	45	80	85
4–6	50	50	75	60	60	55	80	55
7–10	55	70	75	80	80	80	80	55
Male:								
11–14	70	100	85	95	95	90	120	100
15–18	85	100	100	95	100	90	120	100
19–22	85	100	100	100	100	95	80	55
23–50	85	100	100	95	95	90	80	55
51+	85	100	100	80	80	80	80	55
Female:								
11–14	70	80	85	75	75	75	120	100
15–18	70	80	100	75	75	70	120	100
19–22	70	80	100	75	75	70	80	100
23–50	70	80	100	70	70	65	80	100
51+	70	80	100	70	70	65	80	55
Pregnant	+20*	+40*	+20*	+20*	+25*	+10*	+40*	**
Nursing	+30*	+60*	+40*	+20*	+30*	+25*	+40*	**

*To be added to the percentage for the woman of the appropriate age.

**The increased requirement during pregnancy cannot be met by the iron content of habitual American diets; therefore, the use of 30-60 mg. of supplemental iron is recommended. Iron needs during nursing are not substantially different from those of nonpregnant women, but it's recommended that mothers continue supplementing their iron intake for 2-3 months after childbirth to replenish stores depleted by pregnancy.

Sources: Food and Drug Administration; Food and Nutrition Board, National Academy of Sciences, National Research Council (Revised, 1980).

Sources of Important Nutrients 🍎

Below are lists of a few foods that provide significant amounts of the 8 nutrients for which U.S. Recommended Daily Allowances are available. (See pp. 74–80 for lists of good food sources for the other important nutrients.) The U.S. RDA of protein for a 30–year–old male is 85%. As you can see from the list below, that recommendation can be satisfied with a cup of milk (20%), an ounce of cheddar cheese (15%), and a 3–ounce piece of broiled halibut (50%) or a 3–ounce patty of ground beef (50%).

Food	Amount	% of U.S. RDA
Protein		
Beans, red kidney	1 cup	30
Cheese, cheddar	1 oz.	15
Chicken, broiled	3 oz.	45
Eggs	1 whole	15
Ground beef, broiled	3 oz.	50
Halibut, broiled	3 oz.	50
Milk, whole or skim	1 cup	20
Peanuts, shelled	1 cup	80
Pork chop, lean	3 oz.	60
Vitamin A		
Apricots, dried	1 cup	150
Broccoli, cooked	1 med. stalk	90
Cantaloupe	1 half	180
Carrots, cooked	1 cup	330
Liver, beef	3 oz.	910
Vitamin C		
Broccoli, cooked	1 med. stalk	230
Orange juice, frozen	1 cup	200
Peppers, stuffed	1 med.	120
Strawberries, raw	1 cup	150
Tomatoes, cooked	1 cup	100

Source: U.S. Dept. of Agriculture.

Food	Amount	% of U.S. RDA
Vitamin B₁ (Thiamin)		
Beans, navy, cooked	1 cup	20
Ham, diced	1 cup	45
Oatmeal, cooked	1 cup	15
Peanuts	1 cup	30
Pork chop, lean	3 oz.	60
Sunflower seeds	1 cup	190
Vitamin B₂ (Riboflavin)		
Cheese, cheddar, shredded	1 cup	30
Cheese, cottage	1 cup	35
Ham, diced	1 cup	20
Liver, beef or calf	3 oz.	210
Mushrooms, raw	1 cup	20
Vitamin B₃ (Niacin)		
Chicken, broiled	3 oz.	40
Cod, broiled	3 oz.	15
Ground beef	3 oz.	25
Liver, beef or calf	3 oz.	70
Peanuts	1 cup	120
Peas, green, cooked	1 cup	20
Pork chop, lean	3 oz.	30
Sunflower seeds	1 cup	40
Tuna, canned in water	3 oz.	60
Calcium		
Cabbage, cooked	1 cup	25
Cheese, cottage	1 cup	25
Milk, whole or skim	1 cup	30
Spinach, cooked	1 cup	25
Yogurt, plain	1 cup	30
Iron		
Beans, red kidney	1 cup	25
Clams, canned	1 cup	35
Lobster	1 lb.	20
Pork chops, lean	3 oz.	15
Raisins	1 cup	30
Steak, sirloin, lean	3 oz.	20

◐ Saturated and Unsaturated Fats

Saturated fats. Found in dairy products, meats and animal fats. Too much can *raise* the amount of cholesterol* in the blood.

Monounsaturated fats. Found in vegetable oils. No unique characteristics.

Polyunsaturated fats. Pressed from various seeds, fruits and nuts (corn, soybean, sunflower, peanut, etc.). May help *lower* the amount of cholesterol* in the blood.

Cholesterol is a waxy material produced in the liver and in some of the body's cells. It is used beneficially in many of the body's chemical processes, but too high a blood cholesterol level contributes to the development of hardening of the arteries, the condition that underlies most heart attacks and strokes.

Fat Content

How to calculate the percentage of fat in a product:

1. Locate the number of grams of fat per serving on the label. _____

2. Multiply line 1 by 9 (each gram of fat contains 9 calories). _____

3. Locate the number of calories per serving on the label. _____

4. Divide line 2 by line 3. _____

5. Multiply the result by 100 to get the percentage of fat in the product. _____

The following chart identifies the percentage of saturated, monounsaturated and polyunsaturated fat in various cooking oils, vegetable and animal fats.

Fats and Oils

Food	Total Fat (Percent)	Saturated (Percent)	Unsaturated (Monoun-saturated) (Percent)	(Polyun-saturated) (Percent)
Salad and cooking oils				
Safflower	100	10	13	74
Sunflower	100	11	14	70
Corn	100	13	26	55
Cottonseed	100	23	17	54
Soybean	100	14	25	50
Soybean, specially processed	100	11	29	31
Sesame	100	14	38	42
Peanut	100	18	47	29
Olive	100	11	76	7
Coconut	100	80	5	1
Vegetable fats—shortening	100	23	23	6–23
Margarine, first ingredient on label				
Safflower oil (liquid)—tub	80	11	18	48
Corn oil (liquid)—tub	80	14	26	38
Soybean oil (liquid)—tub	80	15	31	33
Corn oil (liquid)—stick	80	15	33	29
Soybean oil (liquid)—stick	80	15	40	25
Cottonseed or soybean oil (partially hydrogenated)—tub	80	16	52	13
Butter	81	46	27	2
Animal fats				
Poultry	100	30	40	20
Beef, lamb, pork	100	45	44	2–6

Source: U.S. Dept. of Agriculture.

Like other carbohydrates, sugar provides the body with energy. But unlike complex carbohydrates, sugar has no nutritional value. Unfortunately, sugar is not only present where we would normally expect to find it—candy, cakes, pies, desserts—but it's also used in the processing of many other foods—catsup, canned soup, salad dressing, frozen dinners and so on. Sugar, of course, is also plentiful in most breakfast cereals. (See accompanying chart.)

Sugar Content

How to calculate the percentage of sugar in a product:

1. Locate the number of grams of sugar per serving on the label (Listed under "Carbohydrate Information"). _____

2. Multiply line 1 by 4 (each gram of sugar contains 4 calories). _____

3, Locate the number of calories per serving on the label. _____

4. Divide line 2 by line 3. _____

5. Multiply the result by 100 to get the percentage. _____

Breakfast Cereals

Cereal	Percent Sugar
Wheat Germ	0
Granola (without sugar)	0
Cream of Wheat	0
Quaker Oatmeal	0
Quaker Farina	0
Nabisco Shredded Wheat	0
Quaker Oats Puffed Wheat, Rice	0
General Mills Cheerios	4
General Mills Kix	5
Ralston-Purina Rice Chex, Corn Chex	5
Ralston-Purina Wheat Chex	6
Kellogg's Corn Flakes	7
General Mills Post Toasties	7
Kellogg's Special K	7
General Foods Grape Nuts	7
Kellogg's Product 19	11
General Mills Total	11
General Mills Wheaties	11
Kellogg's Rice Krispies	11
General Mills Buckwheat	12
General Foods 40% Bran	13
General Foods Grape Nuts Flakes	13
Quaker Oats Life	14
Kellogg's All-Bran	14
Nabisco Team	14
Kellogg's Raisin Bran	14
Kellogg's 40% Bran	18
Quaker 100 Percent Natural Granola With Brown Sugar and Honey	19
General Foods Fortified Oak Flakes	20
Kellogg's Country Morning Granola With Raisins and Dates	21
Nabisco 100 Percent Bran	21
Quaker Oats Life (cinnamon)	21
Pet Heartland Granola With Coconut	22
General Foods Country Crisp	22
Kellogg's Bran Buds	25
Kellogg's Country Morning	25
C.W. Post Granola, plain	25
Quaker 100 Percent Natural Granola With Apple and Cinnamon	25

Cereal	Percent Sugar
General Mills Nature Valley Granola With Cinnamon and Raisins	25
Pet Heartland Raisin Granola	26
General Foods C. W. Post	28
C. W. Post Raisin Granola	28
Quaker 100 Percent Natural Granola With Raisins and Dates	28
Kellogg's Frosted Mini Wheats	28
General Mills Nature Valley Granola With Fruit and Nuts	29
Kellogg's Cracklin' Bran	29
General Mills Golden Grahams	30
General Mills Cocoa Puffs	33
General Mills Trix	35
General Foods Honeycomb	37
General Foods Alpha Bits	38
General Mills Count Chocula	39
Kellogg's Sugar Pops	39
Kellogg's Frosted Rice	39
Quaker Oats Cap'n Crunch	40
General Mills Crazy Cow (strawberry)	40
Quaker Oats Quisp	40
Kellogg's Sugar Frosted Flakes	41
General Mills Lucky Charms	42
General Foods Fruity Pebbles	43
General Foods Cocoa Pebbles	43
Kellogg's Cocoa Krispies	43
General Foods Supe Sugar Crisp	43
General Mills Frankenberry	44
Kellogg's Sugar Corn Pops	46
Kellogg's Sir Grapefellow	46
Kellogg's Baron Von Redberry	46
Kellogg's Corny Snaps	47
General Mills Crazy Cow (chocolate)	47
General Foods Raisin Bran	48
King Vitamin	50
Kellogg's Froot Loops	53
Kellogg's Apple Jacks	56
Kellogg's Sugar Smacks	56

Source: U.S. Dept. of Agriculture.

Sodium

Each day your body needs only about as much sodium as you'll find in 1 teaspoon of salt (or sodium chloride), which is 40% sodium and 60% chloride. That amounts to about 2,000 mgs. (or 2 g.) of sodium. Because too much sodium in your diet can contribute to high blood pressure (hypertension), physicians recommend restricting sodium intake, including visible salt and sodium hidden in processed foods.

Salt and Sodium Conversions

To Convert	Do This
Grams to milligrams	Multiply weight in grams by 1,000
Sodium into salt (NaCl) equivalent	Milligrams of sodium content ÷ .40 = milligrams of salt
Salt into sodium	Milligrams of salt ×.40 = milligrams of sodium

Fresh vs. Processed Foods

The following chart illustrates the different amounts of sodium in a representative *selection* of fresh and processed foods. Fresh foods have been prepared without salt.

Fresh		Processed	
Beef stew, homemade 1 cup	91 mgs.	980 mgs.	Beef stew, canned 1 cup
Cheddar cheese, natural 1 oz.	176 mgs.	406 mgs.	Pasteurized, processed cheese 1 oz.
Corn, fresh, cooked 1 cup	Trace	384 mgs.	Corn, canned 1 cup
Cucumber, whole 1 lg.	18 mgs.	1928 mgs.	Dill pickle, whole 1 large
Green beans, fresh, cooked 1 cup	5 mgs.	326 mgs.	Green beans, canned 1 cup
Hamburger, lean 3 oz. (1 patty)	57 mgs.	639 mgs.	Hot dog 1 hot dog
Kidney beans, dry, cooked 1 cup	4 mgs.	844 mgs.	Kidney beans, canned 1 cup
Lemon 1 wedge	1 mg.	182 mgs.	Tartar sauce 1 tbsp.
Peas, cooked 1 cup	2 mgs.	493 mgs.	Peas, canned 1 cup
Potato, baked 1 med.	5 mgs.	1095 mgs.	Au-gratin potatoes 1 cup
Shrimp, raw 3 oz.	137 mgs.	1955 mgs.	Shrimp, canned 3 oz.
Tomatoes, fresh, boiled 1 cup	10 mgs.	390 mgs.	Tomatoes, canned, whole 1 cup

Source: U.S. Dept. of Agriculture.

Weight Loss Facts

• The average adult American consumes about 3,200 calories per day.
• 3,500 calories equals one pound.
• 500 fewer calories per day will give you a one-pound-per-week loss. 1000 fewer calories per day will give you a two-pound-per-week loss.

Maintenance Dieting Formulas

To know the number of calories you should eat to maintain your present weight, multiply your weight by
• 12, if you're sedentary,
• 15, if you're moderately active,
• 18, if you're active.

Source: *Successful Dieting Tips,* Bruce Lansky (Meadowbrook Press, 1981).

Calories Burned During Various Activities*

Activity	Calorie Loss Per Hour
Rest and light activity	**50–200**
Lying down or sleeping	80
Sitting	100
Driving an automobile	120
Standing	140
Domestic work	180
Moderate activity	**200–350**
Bicycling (5½ mph)	210
Walking (2½ mph)	210
Gardening	220
Canoeing (2½ mph)	230
Golfing	250
Lawn mowing (power mower)	250
Bowling	270
Lawn mowing (hand mower)	270
Rowboating (2½ mph)	300
Swimming (¼ mph)	300
Walking (3¾ mph)	300
Badminton	350
Horseback riding (trotting)	350
Square dancing	350
Volleyball	350
Roller skating	350
Vigorous activity	**over 350**
Table tennis	360
Ditch digging (hand shovel)	400
Ice skating (10 mph)	400
Wood chopping or sawing	400
Tennis	420
Water skiing	480
Hill climbing (100 ft. per hr.)	490
Skiing (10 mph)	600
Squash and handball	600
Cycling (13 mph)	660
Scull rowing (race)	840
Running (10 mph)	900

*These figures are based on the energy expenditure of a 150–lb. person.

Source: President's Council on Physical Fitness and Sports.

⬤ Dieting

Men 25 and older — Desirable Weights

Height (with shoes on 1-inch heels)		Weight		
Feet	Inches	Small Frame	Medium Frame	Large Frame
5	2	112–120	118–129	126–141
5	3	115–123	121–133	129–144
5	4	118–126	124–136	132–148
5	5	121–129	127–139	135–152
5	6	124–133	130–143	138–156
5	7	128–137	134–147	142–161
5	8	132–141	138–152	147–166
5	9	136–145	142–156	151–170
5	10	140–150	146–160	155–174
5	11	144–154	150–165	159–179
6	0	148–158	154–170	164–184
6	1	152–162	158–175	168–189
6	2	156–167	162–180	173–194
6	3	160–171	167–185	178–199
6	4	164–175	172–190	182–204

Women 25 and older*

Height (with shoes on 2-inch heels)		Weight		
Feet	Inches	Small Frame	Medium Frame	Large Frame
4	10	92– 98	96–107	104–119
4	11	94–101	98–110	106–122
5	0	96–104	101–113	109–125
5	1	99–107	104–116	112–128
5	2	102–110	107–119	115–131
5	3	105–113	110–122	118–134
5	4	108–116	113–126	121–138
5	5	111–119	116–130	125–142
5	6	114–123	120–135	129–146
5	7	118–127	124–139	133–150
5	8	122–131	128–143	137–154
5	9	126–135	132–147	141–158
5	10	130–140	136–151	145–163
5	11	134–144	140–155	149–168
6	0	138–148	144–159	153–173

*Women between 18 and 25 should subtract 1 lb. for each year under 25.

Source: Metropolitan Life Insurance Co., Heath and Safety Education Div.